Margaret,

Enjoy Love's Secret, and open your heart to love.

♡ Annie

Cataloging-in-publication information available through the Library of Congress.

Love's Secret

Live Your Life In Love

ANNIE B. LAWRENCE, Ph.D, CHT, HHP

Sedona Publishers
Sedona, Arizona

Love's Secret

Live Your Life In Love

ANNIE B. LAWRENCE, PH.D, CHT, HHP

Published by Sedona Publishers
460 Harmony Drive
Sedona, Arizona, 86336
Copyright ©2007 Annie B. Lawrence

Table of Contents

foreword

I have worked with Annie in her retreats for the last two years and have witnessed the results of her work. Annie has great integrity and walks her talk.

Love's Secret is a valuable resource to cut connections made in childhood to pain and drama and offers solutions to make new connections to love and happiness. Throughout the book you will be guided to create a vision to act as a road map to keep your relationship on course. Apply the techniques offered and you are guaranteed of long term love and happiness in your relationship. In our world of constant fighting you will benefit by creating more love. In my own book *Inside the Atom* I explain the energy of an atom, and I explain that everything is made of intelligent energy particles. Love is an energy vibration and is the highest energy on the planet. I teach a energy healing technique called *Dual Action Life Force Healing*, and offer medical intuitive readings all over the world. My healings and clearings assist my students and clients to be lifted to higher energy vibrations. In all the work that both Annie and I offer, our intention is to initiate love and thereby assist in lifting the vibration of mother earth. For more information or to contact me visit Annie's website at www.retreatandheal.com

Enjoy *Love's Secret* it will make a difference in your life and relationship.

-Dr. Don Engelhardt

Acknowledgements

My thoughts of you are my inspiration to begin my day and my comfort as each day ends.

This book is dedicated to my beautiful husband and life-partner; I share my life and dreams with him. His love and support are a nurturing flame to my creativity and my life. He has supported me in realizing several of my life dreams. These dreams include opening and directing a holistic school and clinic for eleven years. Creating our current healing center, Retreat and Heal, our loving and supportive marriage, and writing this book. These words are for him. Thank you for supporting our love and partnership.

I know love because of him every moment with him is a past, a present, and a future living my dreams and fulfilling my purpose. With his special love and support, and in his own magical way, he has given my days more richness, joy, and love than most people dream of.

I know what love is, because he shares my life. He is the reason for many of my smiles and laughter, I cherish our friendship. My heart feels safe, loved, and understood when he is near. His kind understanding and gentleness gives me hope, helps me feel grateful, and reassured. I know what love is because thoughts of him gently fill my soul with love and joy.

Each day I am grateful to have him to share my life!

I want to thank my two sons, who have been an inspiration to me since the day they were born. Their bright smiles and warm hearts have brought me more love and happiness than any mom could hope for. I thank my daughter Lorrie for supporting me with the designing of the cover. I thank my grandsons Kai, Joey, and Jake for being bright earth angels teaching me to laugh and play. My grandsons have been a welcomed relief to my writing. I thank my daughter in laws Peggy and Brenda for being loving supportive additions to my family.

I want to thank my large family of nine brothers and sisters. I know it has taken patience, kind understanding, and thinking out side the box to accept and understand me and my different ideas and opinions. You gave me a base to begin my journey.

Thank you, Willma Gore, for reading my book in

rough draft, and encouraging me to complete it. Thank you, Ann Crossman and Jeanne Hopkins, for your help and diligence in editing and proofreading.

Finally, I thank all my friends, students, and clients for the love and support they gave me over the years. I have grown and continue to learn from them and we have gained wisdom together over years of sessions and classes. I am grateful for their trust and their love and the many joyful moments shared. They are my extended family and I am grateful our paths crossed.

Introduction
SHOCKED INTO CONSCIOUSNESS

*C*old and shocked, I opened my eyes to greet my new world that felt strange and unwelcoming. I wondered what I did to get kicked out of my warm and cozy environment. Maybe I outgrew it. I remember beginning to feel cramped. My mommy's tummy had been comfortable most of the time, except for occasional shocks and stabs in my heart. Those electric shocks and stabbing pains weren't so bad compared with the constant fear I feel in my new environment.

I made my way down through constricted muscle bands that ushered me along my mother's birth canal. I feared for my life as each breath felt like a panic attack. Then a sudden slap on my tiny rear blasted me into "consciousness." Bright lights were glaring and sent shock waves throughout my tiny nervous system. I don't think I was ready. Would I have ever been?

Several times I have had a dream of re-entering the world and re-experiencing the trauma. I can still feel the electrical shocks I experienced every time my mom felt hurt, angry, or fearful. Immersed in water and breathing deeply in a therapy session, I vividly recalled the rejection I felt while in my mother's womb. In her mid-forties with nine children, my mom was burned out, and another child was not a welcome thought.

Each night I ask to remember my dreams, and more and more information is presented. Remembering the past can become tiresome and overwhelming, and at times my mind will want to stop. At times, the emotional pain is too much to recapture and takes some time to be integrated into my awareness. It is staggering to think that my connections to love and rejection began as far back as my mom's womb. At first it felt hopeless to repair the damage buried deep in my cells and subconscious mind.

Remembering my pain and my journey, I have been told, will help other people to recapture their emotional pain and heal it. Sharing my story will also help to release my own pain.

For this reason I offer this book. It contains tools and experiences to help heal your pain and trauma. We each have chosen to transcend our pain as part of our spiritual growth and awakening. I hope this information will touch your heart and help you heal your emotional wounds, and regain your own personal power.

Love's Secret Live Your Life In Love is written with a vision and intent to offer you hope and assistance in creating the relationship you have longed for, whether you are young or old. This deep longing for a meaningful and lasting relationship is probably one of your heart's deepest desires.

I am throwing life lines to pull you out of the quicksand of your own fears, beliefs, and patterns that bring pain and suffering. You will find effective ways to create the relationship you have dreamed of, but found it hopeless to create on your own.

I offer easy to apply tools and support to change habits and patterns throughout each chapter. You will learn the secret for choosing love over pain to support the relationship of your dreams, along with a road map to keep you on course.

I will guide you, by sharing my own experiences, along with the failures and successes of many clients and students. Names have been changed to protect the true identities in the stories.

I recommend that you make *Love's Secret*, your manual and use it slowly over weeks or months with your partner. Set aside time to work with each chapter, at least one or two hours every week. Take time to integrate each assignment before moving to the next chapter. If you hit an impasse during your healing journey, look in the last chapter and the appendix for support.

Love's Secret number one
Commit to Love

When love beckons to you follow him,
Though his ways are hard and steep.
And when his wings enfold you yield to him,
Though the sword hidden among his pinions may wound you.
And when he speaks to you believe in him.
Though his voice may shatter your dreams as the north wind lays
waste the garden,
For even as love crowns you so shall he crucify you.
Even as he is for growth so is he for your pruning.
Even as he ascends to your height and caresses your tenderest
branches that quiver in the sun,
So shall he descend to your roots and shake them in their clinging
to the earth.
Like sheaves of corn he gathers you unto himself.
He threshes you to make you naked.
He sifts you to free you from your husks.
He grinds you to whiteness.
He kneads you until you are pliant;
And then he assigns you to his sacred fire,
that you may become sacred bread for God's sacred feast.
All these things shall love do unto you that you may know the
secrets of your heart and in that knowledge become a fragment of
Life's heart.

-KAHLIL GIBRAN

Craving Love—Fearing Love

Bob had just met the woman of his dreams. Based on his past, he was scared to death he would "mess up" again. When Bob first entered my office, he was desperate for answers. He wanted to succeed this time more than anything else in the world. In the past when he made a commitment, his fears surfaced and he compulsively began sabotaging himself.

This time he wanted things to be different, not by chance, but because he had a plan and tools to deal with fear of intimacy. He was terrified of love which kept him "commitment phobic," but had never realized his patterns. During our sessions he discovered his fear, and felt a deep relief that he could heal. In the past he had spent his time consumed with searching for the "one," the perfect mate.

Face the Fear

In this chapter you will find the secret for dealing with fear of intimacy and commitment and the underlying fears that can keep you caught in the swinging doors of toxic relationships.

Love's Secret Number 1 is to make a commitment to your own healing. You can then be a support within the relationship for healing your issues as a couple. This chapter explores what commitment means and why you or your mate might be commitment phobic. You will find solutions to overcome the phobias and tools to build new habits to make love. Your commitment to your own inner-healing will build a base for a happy, long-term, loving relationship.

Exercises for journaling and inner-reflection are included throughout the book.

These exercises are intended to connect you with your inner wisdom, and find answers to create the life and relationship that you have longed for.

Quiet inner-reflection through journaling allows ideas and hidden inner-desires to bubble up from within.

Once you have your inner answers on paper, you can examine them and focus your energy to create your heart's desire.

Why Make a Commitment?

In the past Bob would make commitments. In fact, he had been engaged four times and had yet to make it to the altar. Each time as the date approached, he found himself making other things more important and pushing his fiancé away. He convinced himself that she was not the "one". Eventually either he or his fiancé canceled the wedding plans.

In the past he had never found strength or courage to seek help. He just kept playing the game and trusting that eventually he would get it right. This time he felt there was too much at stake, his internal time clock was ticking, and he needed to get it right.

Once you have a partner with whom to create a loving relationship, it is important to make a commitment. Without this commitment, it is too easy to bail out when deep-core issues, arise. Everyone has core issues; and it is a part of your life lesson, to heal past hurts and trauma. Core issues created in your childhood are the magnetic pull that draws you toward your perfect partner in order to begin your healing journey.

Passion Glazed Eyes

A partner, in the beginning, may seem to be a perfect way to heal all your emptiness and loneliness. Through your passion-glazed eyes, this partner appears to be the answer to all your prayers. In truth, this partner is the answer, but only to take you to the next level of your personal and spiritual growth. It takes a great deal of personal development, an ability to stand in the emotional eye of the storm without reacting to your partner's emotional drama, in order to share a loving relationship.

Core Issues Surface to Be Healed

Bob began to access and address core issues that had kept him stuck longing for love and then pushing it away. In the past, he had successfully convinced himself that it was the women he had chosen and that he couldn't seem to find the right one. His parents and environment modeled emotionally-destructive patterns and skills for relationships. Finally he saw through his fog of denial and hidden fears. I introduced EFT, emotional freedom technique, to shift his stuck emotions. In the beginning Bob was hesitant but was ready and open to try anything. Our sessions of EFT were very successful and gave him confidence that he could face his fears and shift the old trauma.

Bob's past habits had kept him stuck in reaction by shutting down and moving away anytime he began to feel vulnerable. Once the initial passionate stage of a relationship was over, core issues began to surface to be healed.

Core issues are survival skills filled with emotionally destructive and addictive patterns. They are automatic reactions to life habituated and painful, yet feel like a normal part of life. In order to give and receive authentic love, old patterns and self-destructive behavior must be changed. The ego, or subconscious mind, will hang on and protect these destructive patterns of self-protection to the bitter end and continue to justify the behavior.

The Cloak of Denial

Bob never felt like he was reacting. It was always the "women" with whom he was involved. He seemed to pick women who were demanding and needy. It was beyond him why they always seemed to be the same. He had never made the connection that, in order to feel love, he had always created pain. He feared the pain of losing love, as he did when he lost his mom and found himself recreating loss of love over and over.

Self-Created Hell

As long as these old tactics of survival and protection continue to rule and guide your life, they stand in the way of creating a long-term, loving relationship. You may find yourself stuck in protection, and reacting by closing your heart. In this emotionally-destructive game of relating you are unconscious of the origin of your self-created hell and inner torture.

When you were small, you learned to shut down to protect

your heart, because emotional hurt was too painful. As an adult your skills of protection and survival stand in the way of receiving love. When hurt resurfaces, you react immediately by shutting down and moving away from what you perceive as a threat to your survival.

Often, your hurt is so deep and painful and the survival skill so strong that you feel you will die if you don't shut down. It takes a strong commitment to your own healing, to be willing to experience the hurt, and move through the pain with your heart open. Out-dated survival skills cannot survive if your love is to thrive.

Bob's pattern of longing for love and a heart connection kept him seesawing between initial euphoria and drowning in pain for months with the loss of love. At times he had been in so much pain that he had contemplated ending his life. Then he developed the skill to practice EFT on himself and found it gave him instant relief from his self-inflicted pain.

Unacknowledged fears draw your worst nightmare toward you. This fear draws a person who possesses the things that bother you most and may leave you feeling rejected and abandoned.

How I Connected Love to Pain

I grew up in an alcoholic family. I was the youngest of ten children, four sisters, and five brothers. My father was the alcoholic and my mother became totally burned out. My memories of being held and loved were from my father, who was an alcoholic, workaholic, and rageaholic. When my father caught me, age five, and my older brothers engaged in innocent sexual exploration, he shut down his heart. After that incident, I never remember being held or loved by him. Due to the harsh discipline they received from my dad my brothers closed their hearts at the same time. From then on, I denied my sexuality and became very isolated.

This incident influenced my entire future for relationships and how I related to men. I felt dirty. Sex was dirty. I didn't deserve to be loved. I longed to be held and loved but yet I was full of guilt, shame and fear, which caused me to shut my heart and hide my true feelings. When I was attracted to men, they were always addictive personalities, who had a lot of healing to do, that mirrored the healing I needed for myself.

Hidden Beliefs and Fears

Bob learned that he had longed for love since birth. His mom and dad were caught up in their own drama and were emotionally unavailable. Deep in his unconscious mind, he had promised himself that he would never trust women. Another part of his hidden promise was to find the "one," before he made a commitment. His buried promise not to trust women happened when his mom deserted the family and left with another man. He was raised by his dad, and never bonded with his mom, or felt feminine love. His soul longed for a feminine connection but he was terrified to trust it.

Hidden beliefs regarding the opposite sex:

☾ Men or women always leave.

☾ Men or women are manipulators.

☾ You can never trust women or men.

☾ Men want sex without emotional involvement.
After they have gotten what they want, they will leave.

☾ Women use sex to manipulate and control.

Exercise to uncover hidden beliefs:

☾ Journal on how the fear of love is impacting your current relationship.

☾ Be honest as you spend quiet time journaling and listening inside. Set aside at least 30 minutes for each journaling experience.

☾ Write and reflect on beliefs that you might have regarding the opposite sex.

☾ Look at your role models for relationships. How are these role models affecting your life?

☾ How happy are you? Do you know how to be happy?

☾ Do you find it easy to make commitments?

☾ Do you find it easy to follow through with the commitments that you make?

☾ Have you experienced love? Do you know what it feels like to be in love and happy?

❧ Do you sabotage yourself when you feel happy? Do you still need pain and drama to feel loved?

❧ When you find someone you love and feel good around do you end up sabotaging yourself to justify pushing the person away?

❧ Come together with your partner and perhaps a coach or counselor to go over what you have learned.

Commit to Heal Your past!

Bob was feeling better after six months of working together and feeling hope for a bright future. We cleared his "promise" to never trust women, revisited his past through hypnosis, and used EFT exercises to clear his old emotions and pain. New trust and excitement were growing inside him. He could now see himself succeeding.

When you enter a relationship, you feel passion luring you into coupling. In this early stage, you are filled with endorphins coloring your world blissful. It is easy to project a picture which you created in your mind, of your perfect mate. This picture, however, doesn't match the emotional radar that is broadcast from hurt and fear in your subconscious mind and which attracts your mate.

Commit or Abandon Hope

When I first met my life partner, each of us was divorced and we had both decided we would never marry again. Jerry and I were hurt and bruised from past relationships, and believed that we would never find authentic love. However, we continued to visualize and pray for a life partner, hoping for the best outcome. Fortunately we continued to open our hearts and experience relationships, even though it included a lot of hurt and pain along the way.

A deep longing to be with our life partner continued inside us. We wanted to be with the person we had carried in our hearts throughout our life. We were driven by a longing to be with someone who would recognize and accept our authentic selves. When we met we were both terrified.

To long for love is easy, to open our hearts and receive love requires strength and commitment. Fortunately, our inner guidance, passion and mutual attraction were stronger than our deep fears.

Secrets to Heal Your Past

☾ You created a cocoon of armoring and protection in youth as a part of your survival skills.

☾ To experience love, you must release this protection.

☾ Childhood protection and survival skills perpetuate playing victim to your past.

☾ Fear can rob you of giving and receiving love.

Exercise to gain clarity

☾ Light a candle and say a short prayer and ask the highest clarity from your guides and angels.

❧ Set your intentions and be aware of how you "react" to life automatically. Don't judge your reactions just bring awareness to your reactions. Focus on your reactions each day for a week and record them in your journal.

❧ At the end of the week share your insights with your mate.

❧ As you share your insights, be a support for each other's change and growth. Never use the information as a power tool to beat each other up.

Clarify your commitment to your current relationship

Read the following questions and rate your commitment. Use a scale ranging from 1-10 (10 being the highest). Be honest with yourself and your partner. You are building trust with each other. When you commit don't just do it on paper, do it in your heart.

❧ I am committed to this relationship.

❧ I am willing to keep my heart open and speak kindly when my mate is pushing my buttons.

❧ I am willing to reflect within, to find what I want and need, and then ask for it.

❧ I can receive what I want without judgment and expectations.

❧ I am committed to choose love over reaction and habit.

EFT for Clearing Hidden Beliefs

Emotional Freedom Technique (EFT)is an effective tool to clear away emotional patterns and beliefs in the emotional body and energy meridians in your physical body. It was developed by Gary Craig, who has an extensive website with lots of self-help information and many DVD's. You will find a link for his website and videos listed on our website link at: www.retreatandheal.com.

EFT incorporates tapping on points that correlate to energy meridians which correspond to organs and glands. By tapping on these meridians and corresponding points, you move and clear energy that became stuck. EFT, also referred to as emotional energy healing, moves stuck energy. It helps you to find the root of emotional and physical pain and "dis-ease." Tapping clears your energy field. As you tap you repeat phrases of self-love and forgiveness. This allows you to replace old patterns, habits, and thoughts. EFT gives you an anchoring tool to replace your conditioned responses with responses that support health and a happy joyful life. Please visit our website for more information: www.retreatandheal.com.

As you tap you will feel a lightening of the pain or emotional discomfort. This indicates that you are doing the exercise correctly. Before you begin tapping check inside for how you feel about commitment. Use a scale of 0-10 (zero no fear and 10 maximum fear). Ask yourself if you have a fear of commitment. When you think of fear of commitment, hold a scene in your mind in which you committed to love and then experienced pain and disappointment.

❦ **Begin by tapping on the top of the center of your head. Repeat as you tap**, "Even though I crave love and find myself terrified when I feel myself opening my heart to receive love, still I choose to deeply and completely love and accept myself."

☾ **Tap on the area between your eyebrows at the inside edge of each eyebrow, above the bridge of your nose. Repeat as you tap,** "Even though I am really afraid of commitment, and I might have promised myself that I would never get married or make a commitment, still I choose to deeply and completely love and accept myself."

☾ **Tap on the outside corner of each eye. Repeat as you tap,** "This fear of love and commitment, created in my childhood and causing me to react by pushing love away, still I choose to deeply and completely love and accept myself."

☾ **Tap on the outside corner of each nostril. Repeat as you tap,** "These decisions I made as a little (girl or boy) based on the writing on my walls and my past experiences as a child, are just old stories written to create my life journey, and my life lessons. Still I choose to deeply and completely love and accept myself."

☾ **Tap on the center of the upper lip just below your nose. Repeat as you tap,** "These old habit of craving love, and pushing love away, and avoiding commitment, are old habits I created in childhood. I give myself permission to create new habits. Still I choose to deeply and completely love and accept myself."

❧ **Tap on the center of the chin just below the lower lip. Repeat as you tap,** "Even though I may have made a vow to myself that I would never trust (men or women), still I choose to deeply and completely love and accept myself."

❧ **Tap on the top of the chest at the inside of each clavicle or chest bone, just below your chin where your neck meets your chest. Repeat as you tap,** "Even though I long for love and want to create a loving relationship, I am terrified of being vulnerable. These old beliefs and patterns I was conditioned to believe as a child seem to have control over me. Still I deeply and completely love and accept myself."

❧ **Tap just below your underarm in the armpit area in line with the nipple. Repeat as you tap,** "Even though I have beaten myself up with these old beliefs and patterns, still I choose to deeply and completely love and accept myself and give myself permission to release the fear of love and commitment."

Keep working with the EFT and the issue of commitment until you get the "fear of love feelings" level down to zero. If you run into deep work and feel lost and confused, seek support.

This exercise will help you to clarify your deep core issues. You may want to work with someone, one-on-one to learn the pattern of EFT, and to clarify how to release your deeper core issues.

Follow the directions and tap along and surprise yourself

how good it feels. Even though you might at first think it feels silly and it can't possibly do anything, give it a try.

Now that you have clarified how you feel about commitment and cleared away some of the pain and hurts blocking your ability to make a commitment, we can create a relationship commitment.

In the next exercise you will be creating a relationship commitment between you and your partner. Read over the following sample commitment. Take time to write your own commitment from your heart. Make it as simple as you like. Your focus is to build rapport and trust. Let the words flow from your heart and offer it as a gift to your partner. Insert your partner's and your name in the appropriate boxes.

Commit to Love

I, _____, commit to owning and healing my baggage, so I can be emotionally available in this relationship. I am willing to keep my heart open, even when I feel hurt and threatened. In all cases I commit to expressing my feelings, although sometimes I may ask for quiet space to clarify what I am feeling and be present with my pain. I will communicate these feelings in a compassionate manner, resisting my need to project the pain and blame it on _____. When I communicate my feelings, I ask to be heard and acknowledged, even though you may not totally agree or understand.

As much as possible I will examine my need to distance myself and hold myself separate, in order to protect myself from change. I realize I am driven inside to give and receive authentic love and this is my intent and goal. I am a spiritual being having a human experience; I have not yet perfected my skills of relating. My role models and environment modeled destructive patterns of shutting down, which ultimately pushed love away. I acknowledge my life lesson to keep my heart open, in spite of everything modeled to me as a child.

I commit to seeing the love and authentic self in _____. And resist the urges of ego to make myself feel superior and struggle for the feeling of being in control. I commit to sharing the reins of control, building mutual respect for each other, and daily creating a safe space for our mutual growth.

I commit to letting go of the fantasy of being "in love" and to create a new image of authentic love. I commit to co-creating the passion in our relationship and keeping fun and excitement alive. I will be open to the needs of my partner as I make my needs known without demands or expectations. Sex is a beautiful way to express love within a spiritual union and I commit to healing past wounds standing in the way of our union.

I take responsibility for my own healing and I own my inner critics, rather than projecting my criticism onto _____. I commit to look inside when I feel judged and to find the inner critic that habitually hurts and puts me down. As I look outward at my mirror in _____, I commit to go inward when I see things that hurt and cause me pain. I remember each day to give thanks for the love I feel growing inside. Each day I take time to do something for my partner that I know _____ loves. I also give love and experiences I value to myself. I have learned to open my heart to receive as easily as I give.

Within our relationship I create space for myself to be quiet inside and do my own healing. Being whole within fills me, so I may give from a full cup. Rather than disowning myself, I commit to taking care of my body, mind, and spiritual growth. This includes exercise, diet, and meditation, a regime that keeps me in good health and peace of mind. A commitment to my happiness is a commitment to my relationship.

The inner joy I experience is reflected into my relationship and then reflected back inside again. I am choosing to change my old vicious cycles of pain and suffering, and learn to focus on love. I allow myself to feel safe and nurtured by our loving relationship that I co-create. I realize the love I give is equal to the love I receive and vice-versa. I continue to open myself wider and wider to give and receive authentic love. I am grateful.

Love's Secret number two
Clear Beliefs

Essence is emptiness.

Everything else is accidental.

Emptiness brings peace to loving.

Everything else disease.

In this world of trickery.

Emptiness is what your soul wants

    -Rumi

Cut Love's Connection to Pain and Drama

Donna was known as the drama queen. She created a drama out of everything in her life and her biggest dramas were her toxic relationships. She had no idea why her relationships were so toxic.

When she entered my office she even introduced herself as the "queen of drama." However, at thirty-three, the drama was getting tiring and she wanted her dream life with kids and a loving husband. She felt her time running out and was impatient to heal and move forward.

Hidden Beliefs—That Recreate Drama

In this chapter you will deepen your awareness to the emotional work needed individually and as a couple. You will discover how to recognize and change your patterns that have connected love to pain and drama. Feel new inner peace as you learn to bring peace to loving.

Empty Your Emotional Bag

Donna had a "dream life" and she wanted it badly enough to commit to healing her wounds. She just didn't know where to start. She had tried traditional counseling and it hadn't changed her dramas. The numbing drugs prescribed made the drama easier to handle emotionally. The side effects from the drugs motivated her to give them up.

Since her 33rd birthday, she seemed to feel hopeless about creating her "dream life" and the children she desperately wanted. She had hoped that they would be in her life by now, but the men that she had been engaged to eventually ended up being "losers."

We began working with EFT and Hypnotherapy and healing her past wounds. She knew exactly what she didn't want, but couldn't figure out why she kept attracting the same personalities in all the men she dated. Her first homework assignment was to monitor feelings and thoughts that accompanied her toxic feelings. She was amazed to find how much fear and anxiety she felt.

Heart Connections

Love's Secret Number 2 is to empty your mind of hidden beliefs and clear outdated emotional patterns linking love to pain and drama. In this chapter practice our tools and exercises to wipe your slate clean and start from scratch. This leaves you free to create what you want, rather than recreating pain and suffering that your parents and their parents lived. Preprogrammed beliefs and patterns passed to you through your environment and your families are your life lessons. Relationships are the platform for completing these lessons; and they are one of your missions in life.

Insanity is doing the same thing and expecting different results.
  -ANONYMOUS

Donna had been operating out of fear all her life and hoping that someday it would magically change. Recently when she was raging with anger toward herself, she saw the quote above in a magazine article and it all began to make sense.

Facing the toxic thoughts and emotions in her journal was challenging. She had been stuffing her emotional pain for thirty-three years. After each EFT session she noticed a huge shift and a feeling of her burdens lifting. She felt hope growing as we released the stuffed emotions she had been terrified to face.

Each moment lost in anger and resentment is a moment lost forever.

-Annie Lawrence

Donna realized she was her own worst enemy and spent a lot of time angry. She resented her life and the cards she had been dealt. In our culture and society, we have an addiction to many things including emotions, work, sex, passion, food, and relationships. The most destructive culprit that sucks our precious life energy is constant busy-ness.

Constant Movement without Contemplation

Busily moving through her life from job-to-job and relationship-to-relationship, without taking time to look at what patterns was running her life, Donna felt too busy to stop and contemplate. Her self-created misery felt normal. As a child she felt loved and acknowledged only when she was hurt or had trauma in her life. Finally her cocoon of drama and pain became too heavy to bear. Like a tree standing in a forest her dramas were so closely identified as her life, she felt she would lose her identity if she changed. This was the hidden issue driving her to recreate pain and drama.

An inner compulsion recreated pain and drama in order to "reconnect to the feeling" of being loved and cared for. As a child, Donna lived in a home full of chaos, toxic emotions, and pain.

She realized that a very young child within her had

neurologically wired love to pain and drama. This toxic wiring sabotaged her "dream life" and happiness. She was tired of beating herself up by reacting with her outdated habits and reactions.

Through our guidance she practiced awareness and developed discipline to train herself to act in new healthy ways, and to develop new habits. Her new actions and habits were creating new nerve pathways to love and happiness. Donna committed to her happiness and healing every day though journaling which kept her present to create healthy habits.

Quiet time for reflection within

☾ Just before bed, spend five minutes breathing deeply, ask for guidance to find your patterns causing pain and drama. As your answers and insight emerge don't judge the insights that come up.

☾ When you complete your reflection, cuddle each other and resolve to feel your heart connection.

☾ Just before you fall asleep ask for your dreams to reveal the patterns to be healed. Leave your journal near your bed. If you awaken, jot down any awareness from your dreams.

☾ Upon waking, write your feelings and emotions.

Keep a mood journal for a month.

℘ Every day write down which predominant emotion you experience. Notice your reaction to that emotion. What emotions seem to drain your energy?

℘ How does the predominant emotion relate to your childhood environment?

℘ Become aware of the emotions that feel most comfortable. Do you get upset at yourself and perpetuate feelings you don't like and try to push them away or deny the emotion altogether? Is your mate a dumping ground?

℘ What affects your moods? Food, TV, news, family, friends, others?

℘ Do you have a family member who affects your moods? How do you deal with this?

Conquer the Addiction to Negative Thoughts

Focusing on negative thoughts about your partner can be an addictive pattern that brings negative validation. Validating yourself through drama and pain may be your way of feeling connected to love. Drama drowns both inner and outer passion.

Thinking about how your mate doesn't dress the way you like or how he or she throws clothes around, will justify your rejecting them. Pushing him or her away and seeking to validate you, reinforces negative patterns. If he or she left, as a result of your negative validation, you would be miserable and lost. A negative validation habit is strong and it takes diligent effort to break, but your happiness depends on it.

When you find yourself focusing on a fight that you had months ago and how wrong your partner was, stop and refocus your thoughts. You can stay caught in negative reinforcement of pain and drama in order to feel love and push love away the rest of your life.

When you get upset do you hold it in or do you share your feelings in a gentle way and release your anger? Once you commit to your own growth and happiness, you have the greatest gift you can give to your relationship. Staying committed to love is essential to keep the pathways for communication open to create lasting love and passion.

Stinking Thinking

Catch yourself *focusing* on negative thoughts. Keep your heart open and *make a new choice to change your thoughts to love and acceptance.* This empowers you to build inner passion and happiness.

Habits that Destroy Love

Holding onto resentment and stuffing anger are patterns that are destructive to you and your relationship. They are deeply embedded habits and always surface, to be healed once the endorphins from your initial passion have worn thin. Practice awareness and replace the habit of distancing to accepting and acknowledging your partner.

Acknowledgement builds love and passion.

If you define yourself by your old conditioning, it will be a challenge to replace the destructive habits that drown passion and destroy love.

In order to create love and intimacy in your relationship, you must practice awareness, and develop discipline to choose new thoughts and develop new habits.

You May Crave Intimacy—Yet Push It Away

As Jerry and I moved beyond the euphoric endorphin stage of our relationship and settled into the deep healing that we came together to do, we experienced a rough first year.

I didn't want to take the next step and get married. Jerry did. He was hurt that I didn't want to make this commitment. It caused some hurt and created some distance between us for a while.

As I searched my heart and looked more deeply to find what I was afraid of, I realized I was terrified of intimacy. I had searched my whole life to find my life partner, someone who could be steadfast and give me love. Yet, as I searched my heart, I realized I was afraid of receiving what I had been searching for. It was hard for me to accept, but I became painfully aware that all my old fears and survival skills were standing in my way of being in love and being loved.

After a lot of soul searching, prayer and meditation, I was guided to give love a chance. My inner guidance directed me to commit to my own growth and own my hurt and pain. I learned I could survive my buried hurt and pain, keep my heart open, and allow myself to receive the love that I had longed for all my life. It was welcome relief, to find that the pain of shutting down is greater than moving through old hurt stored from childhood.

I had created a vicious cycle of longing for love, yet moving away when it came close to me. What an eye-opener to reflect on past relationships and realize I had always been with and attracted to men who were emotionally unavailable. I had never met a mate who had been willing to make a commitment to healing our hurt, or had skills to heal our issues. This was a mirror of my own hurt and avoidance of hurt.

Clear the Fear of Intimacy

Each day after journaling, practice EFT to clear away the stuck emotional energy patterns that have surfaced. With each practice, EFT will become more powerful and the words and phrases will surface from inside to clear away your old blocks and conditioning.

If you get stuck on a deep core issue, give us a call or seek help from a professional who offers EFT. Visit our website for contact information www.retreatandheal.com

Before you begin, always check in with the emotions you feel, based on a 0-10 scale. Hold a mental picture of a past emotional time when you experienced a fear of intimacy. It could be as an adult or as a child. Go with whatever surfaces first. Remember to watch for a release of the pain or emotional discomfort. This indicates that you are shifting the stuck emotional energy.

☙ **Begin by tapping on the top of the center of your head.** **Repeat as you tap,** "Even though I may have pain and drama linked to love, still I choose to deeply and completely love and accept myself."

☙ **Tap on the area between your eyebrows, at the inside edge of each eyebrow, above the bridge of your nose. Repeat as you tap,** "Even though I may feel I have to experience pain in order to feel loved, still I choose to deeply and completely love and accept myself."

☙ **Tap on the outside corner of each eye. Repeat as you tap,** "This old feeling of needing to be hurt in order to open my heart to love that I created in childhood, causing me to push love away. Still I choose to deeply and completely love and accept myself."

☙ **Tap on the outside corner of each nostril. Repeat as you tap,** "These decisions I made as a little (girl or boy) based on the writing on my walls and my past experiences as a child, are just old stories written to create my life journey and create my life lessons. Still I choose to deeply and completely love and accept myself."

☾ **Tap on the center of the upper lip just below your nose. Repeat as you tap,** "These old habits of pushing love away and yet craving love and intimacy caused me to shut down my heart. Just habits, not who I am, I am not my habits, I am more than my habits. I can take my power back from my habits and choose to create new habits. Still I choose to deeply and completely love and accept myself."

☾ **Tap on the center of the chin just below the lower lip. Repeat as you tap,** "Even though I may have made a vow to myself that I would never open my heart and allow myself to be vulnerable, still I choose to deeply and completely love and accept myself."

☾ **Tap on the top of the chest at the inside of each clavicle or chest bone, just below your chin where your neck meets your chest. Repeat as you tap,** "Even though I long for love and dream of creating a loving relationship, I am terrified of creating a living hell through a life and relationship filled with pain and drama. These are old beliefs that I was conditioned to believe as a child and seem to have control over me; still I deeply and completely love and accept myself."

☾ **Tap just below your underarm in the armpit area in line with the nipple. Repeat as you tap,** "Even though I have beaten myself up with these old beliefs and patterns, still I deeply and completely love and accept myself and choose to release the fear of opening my heart to receive love. I give myself permission to feel safe to create new patterns and habits that support keeping my heart open and accepting love."

Listen closely to yourself within as you tap, and gain awareness of your inner knowing. Your inner truth and awareness will surface phrases to heal your blocked energy. Your own words and phrases will bubble up as you become more comfortable with the process. Take those words and phrases and insert them in the pattern above or tap where you feel guided. The more you work with the pattern, the more comfortable you will become and deeper healing will result.

EFT is like yoga or meditation: without practice, it will feel awkward. With practice you will gain more confidence, deeper clarity, and better results.

Love's Secret number three
DEVELOPING TRUST

*D*eveloping trust for Love is like developing a taste for *expensive wine. Open your senses and treat yourself to an indulgence your soul has longed for.*

-ANNIE LAWRENCE

Release Your Control Addiction

Helen was a control freak. She had a compulsion to take care of everyone else's needs, but she didn't know why, and didn't have a clue as to what her own needs were. Somewhere in her over-burdened schedule of controlling people around her, she had lost her own identity.

In her partnership she was in control of everything: money, children, household, and their lifestyle. Her husband earned the money and she spent the money: she paid bills and provided all the necessities. Were they happy? They were busy from sun up to sun down, and neither of them had taken time to answer that important question.

Love's Secret Number 3 is to develop trust within you and within the relationship. In this chapter you will learn tools to release your addiction to the feeling of control and learn to recognize your own needs.

A Contract for Spiritual Partnership

In the beginning of their marriage, Helen and Dan were very passionately in love; at least that is what they remember. That was twelve years ago, and since that time they had lost touch with their passion, both within the relationship and individually, they were just living from day to day. Each had believed that they were meant to be together. They felt a special connection.

When you begin to see a different person than when you first met, the spiritual work of relationship has begun. This change in perception is usually initiated by the introduction of core issues and emotional baggage, hidden wounds you carry and try so desperately to avoid.

Terrifying monsters are locked away in individual emotional closets, with no conscious desire to release them. You make a commitment on a deeper spiritual level to assist each other in healing through your partnership.

The secret is to heal your individual wounds, have fun, keep your love and passion alive, deepen your trust, and keep lines of communication open. In this chapter you will find tools for owning you addiction to control, and learn tools for releasing the feeling of being in control, in order to make love.

Auto-Pilot—Developing Control

Neither Helen nor Dan had thought about having a power struggle at the beginning of their marriage. They just settled in and began to live life. Helen became pregnant three months later, ended her intended career, and became a fulltime mom. It seemed only natural to take care of everything in the home and keep it under control. She never thought about needing to feel in control, and Dan never wanted control of those things.

Conquering your ego's need to be right and the constant power struggle over the need to feel in control is essential to a lasting, loving relationship. What is it that you need to control or have the feeling of controlling? Many times as a child you wanted the feeling of being in control and learned negative habits to manipulate that feeling. In order to keep passion alive and growing with your partner, you must be aware of how your need to feel in control is sabotaging your relationship.

Feels Like Control—"Being" Controlled

By following the patterns set up by their parents, Helen and Dan fell into patterns that felt natural. Both of their families had dysfunctional households, with the mother in control of the house and the father in control of the money. In Helen's model of motherhood, her mother controlled everything by "doing" everything herself in the home. Dan on the other hand had a father who went to work and had dinner on the table waiting for him when he returned. Getting through life had been Dan and Helen's focus. They never developed habits of sharing responsibility, developing trust, or keeping their love alive.

Fear of being vulnerable and maintaining the feeling of being in control is the basis of many co-dependent relationships. Falling into old habits modeled to you as a child may give you the feeling of control. In the end you are being controlled by "old habits." Doing things to maintain the feeling of being in control shows up in your life in many ways.

This may include being in control of laundry, driving, groceries, money and finances, and housekeeping. Normally in this type of partnership, one person will become submissive and allow the other to maintain feeling in control. One day the submissive wakes up and feel controlled or the controller wakes up and feels resentment.

Control Collides with Change

Dan and Helen's relationship was changing, not because they wanted it, but because life has its way of initiation. Helen was offered a chance to re-establish her intended career and she wanted to seize the opportunity. This threw everything into change.

Helen felt over-burdened: Dan didn't like doing housework because he had never had to. Helen had trained the kids that mom would handle everything. Helen felt resentment that she didn't feel supported by the family. Dan and the children didn't want things to change; they liked being taken care of. Years of being on auto-pilot and living from day to day, had just collided with change.

Once the habits and patterns of a partnership are established and have been in place for years, it is a challenge to change. It takes deep commitment both to individual growth and the partnership.

You must each be equally committed to creating a happy partnership that will meet the needs of each partner both individually and as a couple. It is a rocky road to change old patterns and habits. Once habits are established it feels like facing death to change. However, change is required whether you commit to an existing relationship, or begin a new one.

Compassion and Compromise

In the beginning Helen had loved the feeling of being the giver to everyone around her. As she became more addicted to maintaining her feeling of being in control, she had abandoned herself and lost her passion for life.

Dan and Helen felt lost and didn't know how to regain peace. They were introduced to me through a mutual friend. Helen was not willing for things to remain the same, which is what the rest of the family wanted. I taught them to speak with compassion from their hearts and to be empathetic listeners. They were able to recognize the sacrifice that Helen had made for each of them and they developed new habits of taking responsibility for their own needs. Our coaching sessions offered them tools to negotiate and create a plan to restore peace within their family.

Secrets for Owning Your Power

☪ Own your power and give up your addiction to the feeling of being in control.

☪ Watch your habits change by controlling your thoughts and emotions.

☪ Learn to be happy in each moment and watch your inner passion and inner peace grow.

☪ Stop the struggle to feel in control and feel your happiness and energy explode.

☪ Redirect your energy from struggling to feel in control into building your dream relationship.

Your Partner is Your Mirror

Your partner is your mirror and barometer to show you where you are focused. Each day look at your partner and notice what you see. Do you see love staring back or do you see rejection? If you see rejection, get in touch with what you are rejecting about yourself, and learn to love yourself and your partner.

Choosing new thoughts and creating new habits will

allow you to keep your heart open when you scrape deep wounds from childhood. At first, it is a challenge to feel safe when you are in pain, to allow your partner to be with you, and keep your hearts open to love. Tightening your body, negative habits, and toxic emotions become identified as who you are. Replace them with healthy habits and feel your love grow.

The part of you that feels validated by feeling rejected and creates drama to feel loved will need to die in order to choose love.

Rewiring for Love

℃ Start each day by focusing on what you love about your partner.

℃ See the best in your partner and you are choosing to see the best in yourself.

℃ Loving him or her nourishes your soul.

℃ Keep your heart open and heal pain and trauma, clear emotional blocks, and rise to a new level of intimacy.

℃ This is the groundwork for deepening your heart connection and building new nerve pathways to love.

EFT to Focus on Love

Set aside 15-30 minutes each day and reflect in your designated sacred space. Turn off all phones, and outside disturbance. Set up a space that supports your journey inside. This space promotes inner peace and inner reflection.

Practice deep breathing for five minutes to gain access to your inner guidance. As you follow your breath, give yourself permission to travel to your deep, inner space. Each time you repeat your ritual, you will find it easier to travel deep inside. Notice where your mind goes and what you want to focus on.

After noticing where your mind naturally goes, pull it back and choose to focus on love for your partner for 5 minutes.

Write down all the things you love about your partner. Focus on your list for five minutes. This exercise will act as an anchoring tool for love and builds trust within your relationship.

Use the following EFT exercise for releasing old conditioning that creates an addiction to the feeling of being in control. Practice this exercise and notice your inner reactions and emotional responses. Write down your reactions and new awareness that arise. This will allow you to replace my words and phrases with your own.

☾ **Begin by tapping on the top of the center of your head. Repeat as you tap,** "Even though I protect my heart from feeling vulnerable by maintaining a feeling of being in control, still I choose to deeply and completely love and accept myself."

☾ **Tap on the area between your eyebrows, at the inside edge of each eyebrow, above the bridge of your nose. Repeat as you tap,** "Even though I maintain my feeling of control by focusing on everyone else, still I choose to deeply and completely love and accept myself."

℞ **Tap on the outside corner of each eye. Repeat as you tap,** "This old fear of being vulnerable and being hurt, was created in my childhood and is causing me to lose myself and my identity, still I choose to deeply and completely love and accept myself."

℞ **Tap on the outside corner of each nostril. Repeat as you tap,** "Old decisions that I made as a little (girl or boy) based on the writing on my walls and my past experiences as a child, are just old stories written to create my life journey, and create my life lessons. Still I choose to deeply and completely love and accept myself."

℞**Tap on the center of the upper lip just below your nose. Repeat as you tap,** "These are old habits of focusing my attention and love outward to the people around me and denying my own needs, in order to maintain a feeling of control. Old habits created by a little (girl or boy) who never felt safe. Just habits, not who I am; I am not my habits; I am more than my habits. I can take my power back from my addiction to the feeling of being in control, and choose to create a new feeling of being safe. Still I choose to deeply and completely love and accept myself."

℞ **Tap on the center of the chin just below the lower lip. Repeat as you tap,** "Even though I may have made a vow to myself that I would maintain this feeling of being in control, and never allow myself to be vulnerable, still I choose to deeply and completely love and accept myself."

☙ **Tap on the top of the chest at the inside of each clavicle or chest bone, just below your chin where your neck meets your chest. Repeat as you tap,** "Even though I long to feel safe and dream of creating a peaceful life, I am terrified of creating a life filled with chaos and drama, still I deeply and completely love and accept myself."

☙ **Tap just below your underarm in the armpit area in line with the nipple. Repeat as you tap,** "Even though I have beaten myself up with this old belief and pattern, and lost my own identity, still I deeply and completely love and accept myself and choose to release the fear of letting go, I give myself permission to create new patterns and habits of feeling safe and building trust within myself."

Practice the EFT exercise with awareness of your inner dialog. Write down any "Aha's!" that surface and keep working alone or with your mate until you have your feelings of fear of vulnerability or need to control down to zero.

Journal to Focus on Love

☙ "I am committed to becoming aware of conditioning that may have love connected to pain." Think of love and pain and any connections you might have made as a child. It is easy to say you are committed. It is harder to do the healing.

❧ "I am committed to my own growth and to developing the discipline to change my thoughts and habits to develop a healthy loving relationship." Post this note in your work area and on your mirror in your bathroom.

❧ "I commit to deal with the emotions that I feel uncomfortable with: anger, fear, guilt, sadness, rejection, and shame." Love and relationships will bring up these emotions to be healed. Spend a day focusing awareness on each of the above emotions to find your comfort level.

❧ "I consciously choose to react in healthy ways and create new habits." Keep your journal for a week and notice your reactions to emotional pain. Be honest with yourself. You cannot heal otherwise. Are you beginning to create new habits? The key is to find the payoff or negative gratification for old habits. Once you have admitted to yourself why you like to hold on to negative gratification of pain, you can choose to quit. It may be that you need to make sure that your partner will stay, no matter what you say or do. Like when you create a fight and get upset, and later notice you were overreacting and pushing your mate away. You begin to notice a pattern of creating a fight just to help yourself feel more connected and to assure yourself that they will not leave.

❧ "I recognize my patterns of shutting down." Take this statement and focus on it for a day. In the beginning, you will feel frustrated if you react, and you might feel out of control as you let go. Be patient with yourself, and love yourself even when you find yourself reacting with old patterns.

❧ "I love making new decisions and creating new habits, even when I feel uncomfortable with the change the new habits bring." Practice being gentle as you learn to react differently to life.

❧ "I choose to change how I identify myself and how I react to life." Old habits and reactions felt like they were protecting you, but were causing you pain and despair.

❧ "I choose to rise above my ego's negative gratification to pain and take my power back from my negative reactions." Establishing new habits takes awareness, then stopping the thought patterns. Say words like "cancel-cancel" when you notice the old thoughts running in your head. Do some EFT to release emotions and patterns that arise.

❧ "I choose to love and accept myself." Always notice your inner reactions when you say positive statements.

❧ "I choose love and to create habits associated with love and acceptance." Stop reacting and stop connecting your neurological pathways to pain.

Love's Secret number four
Open Your Heart

A *heart afraid of opening to give or receive will push both love and money away.*

-ANNIE LAWRENCE

Healing Money Fears

Meg grew up in the Midwest and was the youngest of seven children. She knew what it was like to go to bed hungry, and made a vow that some day she would have lots of money. Meg took her first job at age nine; she convinced her mom to allow her to take a paper route. Hand-me-down clothes and shoes composed her tattered wardrobe and were a constant embarrassment. She was determined to change her plight. Eagerly she saved her money, and full of excitement, bought her first new outfit that fit perfectly. She felt like a million bucks! From this point forward Meg created her own money and learned to be very independent. Meg loved her independence and didn't like to be told how to spend her money.

Clear Toxic Patterns Regarding Money

Love's Secret Number 4 is to open your heart to love and money. In this chapter we will look at your history from childhood and the beliefs you were taught about money and security. You may have been taught that people who have money have control. As a child who had no money or control you may have made a decision that you would never struggle for money when you grew up.

Decisions about money may have created a person who is very thrifty and frugal. On the other hand your mate may have made the decision that when he or she made their own money they would spend it for whatever they wanted. This pattern could be one of spending as quickly as money touches their hands and never feeling good about being on a budget. If a couple has different value systems, this creates power struggles and competition. It will never create teamwork until a compromise is reached. In this chapter you will find tools to clear your beliefs and blocks to opening your heart to create a solid foundation for love.

Determination to be Financially Independent

Meg bought her own duplex at age twenty-eight and became a young investor. She didn't have the money or encouragement to enter college but was looking for a way to get ahead. Real Estate looked like a way to create some extra cash flow. Meg wasn't afraid to try new things. She didn't buy into the stereotypical jobs for women. Most of her friends warned that she was getting into something that required too much work and it could lead her to financial ruin. She wasn't afraid of hard work, or stepping out and reaching for what she wanted.

Meg preferred to look at the positive side of the coin; real estate could be her ticket to financial freedom. Even though, she had climbed the ladder to shift manager, the job paid only $12 an hour. Meg had worked at her local grocery store for seven years. She accepted all the overtime and extra shifts that opened up, but still she found it hard to save money and get ahead. Her new car consumed a large part of her paycheck. The party scene didn't appeal to her, so her social life was pretty simple. Most of the men she had met in her social circle didn't appeal to her. She found them immature and felt that they lacked motivation.

Strong Motivation to Succeed

Personal goals kept Meg focused and helped her to purchase her own home. Not many of her friends had any goals or cared whether they owned or rented their home. She moved often as a child, and her mom never owned a place to call home. Meg had vowed to herself she would never end up in that predicament. Real estate seminars and other investors had given her the vision and hope of buying a home before she was thirty.

At the seminar she heard that a duplex could be a good first-time investment. Meg found an older duplex that needed some fix-up. It had a for-sell-by-owner sign in the front yard. Meg had driven by many times. One day she stopped by on impulse and found the owner home. The owner was anxious to sell, and willing to carry the note with a $5000 down payment and a five-year balloon. Meg was ecstatic; her dream had come true and she was on her way. Now she owned her own home and rented the other side and paid less rent for more space.

A Chance for Love

Two months after buying her new home, Meg met Paul. Paul had been coming into the grocery store for months and always chose Meg's lane to check out. He chatted and seemed very friendly. Although very frightened inside, he finally got up the courage to ask Meg for a date. Meg was surprised, but accepted. Paul had grown up in Tokyo and moved to the Boston area when he was twelve. Recently he had moved to Cottonwood, Arizona, where Meg had lived since she was sixteen. Her social life had been somewhat solitary. It consisted of hiking and biking with little chance of meeting the person of her dreams.

Paul Enters Meg's Life

Meg and Paul found themselves very attracted to each other; this seemed like the relationship they each had dreamed of. Every day found them together: for dinner, and usually included overnight. The next logical step was to make a deeper commitment and move in together; an added benefit would be the money saved by combining rents.

Both had grown up poor and each had dreams of getting ahead financially. Meg, however, was a very independent woman who had been on her own since she was seventeen. Paul had grown up in a culture of women being submissive and always giving their husbands power to make family decisions. Six months into the relationship, security issues and cultural differences began to surface and threaten their future.

Money Issues Surface

As a couple, they valued each other and admired the very qualities that were pushing them apart. Their cultures were different, and were causing them to butt heads, as their money issues came to the surface. They wanted to continue their relationship but realized they didn't have a role model or know how to create it. They decided to attend a weekend retreat and learn some new skills for working out their differences. Before attending, they were to do some journaling and soul-searching. Meg and Paul were asked to find what it was that bothered them about their relationship. Then create a vision of how they wanted their relationship to be.

Independence Pushes Love Away

Paul found that it made him feel very hurt and angry when

Meg didn't need him to take care of her. He found that his self-esteem was wrapped up in being in control of the money and the checkbook. He had been married once for eight years, and it all seemed to roll smoothly until the tragic and painful ending. He had chosen an Asian girl, who was very submissive and wanted a husband to take care of her. He found it very easy to take care of her and their money. She had been killed three years ago in a car accident.

Meg was his first relationship since and also his first relationship outside his Asian culture. After deep soul searching, Paul found that he didn't really want to have all the control of their money; he was just used to that. He was very attracted to Meg's independence, but something inside him still wanted to control that. It was a real dichotomy for him; it felt like something bigger inside him wanted to control what he felt attracted to. It almost felt like he was cracking up. As he tried to look deeply at his need to control, he felt confused and scared.

Control Issues Surface

Meg had never been with anyone who wanted to control her. She had never allowed anyone to stay in her life if they exerted the least amount of control. She had witnessed her mom being controlled by men and vowed to herself that she would never stay in a similar situation. She had fantasized about a harmonious relationship and having a husband who respected her for her independence.

Now it seemed she had allowed herself to fall in love with a person who was a control freak. She admired Paul's stability and his commitment to a relationship that was good for both of them. He was willing to look for ways to create a healthy relationship and he was willing to put in the work to make it happen. Meg realized this was hard to find in men of her age. Most of the men Meg had dated were the "love 'em and leave 'em kind." They wanted to party and have a good time and then move on to a new encounter.

Outside Support

Meg valued Paul's commitment to their relationship but found it difficult to tolerate his need to control her and their money. Paul realized that this relationship would never be what he considered a normal relationship. But he loved Meg and wanted to do whatever it took to make it work. Our weekend retreat helped them to move through their tricky maze of reaction that had set them against each other and became very volatile. They took turns sharing their feelings, while the other person listened with an open heart and mind.

In our life-coaching sessions, they realized that their old patterns and habits were a roadblock to a relationship that could be mutually rewarding. As they listened and communicated from their hearts, they realized that they each had a belief system that was in direct conflict with the person they loved. They also realized that they were conscious enough to make new decisions, based on their present situation.

Staying Committed When the Urge is to Flee

Meg began to see clearly that Paul was not like any of the men who had controlled and manipulated her mother. As she reviewed the last few months, she saw that Paul treated her with respect and valued her as a woman and partner. However, when Paul tried to control her money, she wanted to run as far away from him as possible.

Paul didn't like it when Meg went to her real estate workshops or spent money on books and tapes. When this subject came up, Meg shut down and began to make plans for having him move out. She began to justify, that she didn't need a man or his control.

Her thoughts would begin to spin out of control and she assured herself she was happier on her own. She then began to visualize herself on her own and pursuing her goals more easily. Meg quickly noticed that as soon as she allowed her mind to react to old fears and focus on thoughts of distancing and separation, she and Paul had a big fight. She was torn between loving Paul and wanting to be with him, and wanting to pursue her dreams and freedom.

Heart Expressions

Meg shared her dilemma from her heart. Paul had never realized how committed she was to her dream of financial freedom and independence. Meg had been afraid to share her dream with Paul about owning real-estate rentals and becoming financially independent.

Paul had his own business and didn't have time to devote to anything beyond his business and their relationship. He felt that his business could provide everything that the two of them and their family would ever need. That was not enough for Meg. Based on her past and all the men her mom had been with, she had vowed never to put all of her hopes and dreams into a man.

Negotiating Solutions

Paul was beginning to understand where Meg was coming from and why she was against putting all their money into his business. He had seen it as their ticket to financial freedom. Meg couldn't trust that, and felt that she would be giving up her dream for Paul's dream. Putting all their money into Paul's business was in direct conflict with an inner vow she made. She felt that if she put all of her money into his business and it didn't work out, she would be back to square one with her life's dream.

Reacting to Life Based on the Past

Meg had never seen her mom stay with a man for more that three years, most of the men would move on. Paul saw his commitment being for the rest of his life. He didn't understand why Meg couldn't feel that and trust it.

They agreed that this was the thing that bothered them most. It had become the topic of their fights the last three months, and they could not seem to find a compromise. As their coach, I asked them to stay in their hearts and to feel what the other person was feeling and saying. They agreed to set their problem aside for one night and to be with each other.

Holding Images of Love

They agreed to remember the first night they had spent together and to allow themselves to give their love to each other from that space. We set an intention to seek their answers inside. Each of them asked for a compromise to be revealed.

Paul had agreed to seek the stillness for an answer if Meg would sit with him in meditation that evening. Meg agreed and they sat with each other and connected on a soul level as they practiced tantric meditation. Paul practiced tantra and sometimes it seemed threatening to Meg, but this evening she agreed to be open to it.

A Commitment to Love

The next morning they came back together and we shared their insights from their dreams. Meg had received a visionary dream in which she saw her life with Paul in the future and they had a family. She saw that their business had prospered and with that new prosperity she now had enough money to invest in many rentals. She also saw in the dream that the rentals had created the extra cash flow to allow her to be a stay-at-home mom and she saw herself being very happy.

Paul had a new openness to allowing Meg to pursue her interest in real estate. He had seen his control in a new light and realized that he wanted Meg to have her own interests. He felt a new, deeper commitment and love for Meg and wanted to show it to her by being more supportive of her pursuit of financial independence.

By focusing on their deep love and commitment they had lifted the vise that had them caught in arguments and competition for control. It felt as if the mud had been wiped clean and they could again see the person they had been attracted to at the start of the relationship.

Connected to Love—Negotiating Differences

Meg and Paul deepened their heart connection. They learned to communicate and negotiate for what they valued in a relationship, while keeping their hearts open. Their love, respect, and commitment helped them to compromise and feel good about the solutions they negotiated. Paul found that as he looked closely at Meg's past habits, he trusted her to share the responsibility of their money. It required compromise and changing old habits, but the rewards were worth the effort.

Feeling Safe to Open to Love

The weekend had begun with miles of hurt and wanting to get as far away from each other and the conflict as possible.

Their love and commitment had been the inspiration to book the retreat and then follow through. Both agreed that they were glad they had made the time and spent the money to attend.

If they had continued with old beliefs based on the past they would have missed the chance to build the lasting relationship and family they each deserved. They would have missed the chance to experience the beautiful children that Meg saw in her dream. With their hearts open to each other again, and with renewed love and commitment, they set a date for their marriage. With their unified vision as their guide and realistic goals for their future, they felt confident to begin their journey together.

A Financial Strategy for Teamwork

❧ Create a budget and learn to negotiate your differences; rather than needlessly abandoning ship before finishing the work you came together to heal.

❧ Learn to negotiate from your heart and don't react to differences and disagreements by feeling rejected and shut down.

❧ The relationship you have with money comes from your conditioning as a child. Until you realize your habits and conditioning about money, these money beliefs control you.

❧ Once you have created a vision that incorporates each persons needs, you are able to create a budget that creates a financially-stable lifestyle and fosters inner peace.

🌜 Make goals and prioritize a budget that supports your vision and life style.

🌜 Make sure the lifestyle is easy, simple to maintain, and covers each person's needs.

🌜 Once negotiated and on paper, it is simple to prioritize your goals and create your lifestyle.

🌜 It can be fun and exciting to make goals and follow a budget.

🌜 By following your budget you will begin to build a strong financial base together, and avoid power struggles regarding money.

Clear Money Fears

Use EFT for clearing old beliefs and patterns about money and the blocks that may be keeping you stuck in poverty consciousness and struggle. Think about what you want in life. Hold the picture of having these things in your life and notice your feelings. Do you fear having what you want? Do you have a belief that you don't deserve what you want? Do you feel you have to push and struggle to achieve your goals and dreams? Below, you will find words and phrases for releasing some of the most common blocks to creating your heart's desire. When you listen and find your own words, insert them into the EFT script.

🌜 **Begin by tapping on the top of the center of your head. Repeat as you tap,** "Even though I may have a belief that I don't deserve money and prosperity, still I choose to deeply and completely love and accept myself."

❧ **Tap on the area between your eyebrows, at the inside edge of each eyebrow, above the bridge of your nose. Repeat as you tap,** "Even though I was poor as a little (girl or boy), wore hand me down clothes, and have experienced life as a constant struggle and I can't see anything else in my mind. Still I choose to deeply and completely love and accept myself."

❧ **Tap on the outside corner of each eye. Repeat as you tap,** "These are old fears of poverty, and create bills and struggle, while I long for an abundant life. These old beliefs I created cause me to feel hopeless and overwhelmed. Still I choose to deeply and completely love and accept myself."

❧ **Tap on the outside corner of each nostril. Repeat as you tap,** "These decisions I made as a little (girl or boy) based on the writing on my walls and my past experiences as a child, are just old stories written to create my life journey, and create my life lessons. Still I choose to deeply and completely love and accept myself."

❧ **Tap on the center of the upper lip just below your nose. Repeat as you tap,** "This old fear of poverty and struggle is connected to inner pain and feelings of hopelessness. Old habits created by a little (girl or boy) who longed to have an easier life, are just habits, not who I am, I am not my habits; I am more than my habits. I can take my power back from my addiction to struggle and my longing for an easier life. I can choose to create a new feeling of being safe, to experience a life of abundance. Still I choose to deeply and completely love and accept myself."

✆Tap on the center of the chin just below the lower lip. Repeat as you tap, "Even though I may have made a vow to myself that I would never allow myself to get caught in struggle and hopelessness, still I choose to deeply and completely love and accept myself."

✆Tap on the top of the chest at the inside of each clavicle or chest bone, just below your chin where your neck meets your chest. Repeat as you tap, "Even though I long to feel happy, joyful and live an abundant life, but I am terrified of being lost in poverty, struggle, and failure. This old pattern of believing I can have what I want, but being terrified of failure inside, is a pattern that repeats, and creates struggle and anxiety. Still I deeply and completely love and accept myself."

✆Tap just below your underarm in the armpit area in line with the nipple. Repeat as you tap, "Even though I have beaten myself up with this fear of failure while recreating failure, still I deeply and completely love and accept myself and choose to release the fear of believing in myself to create success and abundance. I give myself permission to feel safe to create new patterns of success and habits that build success and abundance."

After completing this EFT tapping session, check inside yourself. Test your self with the same scale of 0-10. Hold a scene of failure and struggle in your mind. How much fear do you have of believing you can achieve success? Listen to your inner critic. Keep working either alone or with your mate to bring the score to zero.

Create a Budget

Keep a "Money Journal" for a month

Create a money journal and write down where you spend your money, and how you feel when you spend it.

Notice if you feel good to let the money leave your hands. Or do you resent having to spend your money? This can be especially true if you have child-support or spousal-support payments. Resentment is not a good relationship to have with money. It will push abundance out of your life. Seek out help with your coach, or counselor, to heal the resentment and establish a new relationship with money.

Love your job.

Do you hold a feeling of gratitude for your job, your co-workers, and your paycheck? Look at this as honestly as possible. Write each day for a month on how you feel about each of these topics. If you don't love your work, find ways to accept and enjoy where you are in the moment and seek new ways to create a new job that you can feel passionate about.

At the end of the month tally the results of where you spend your money.

Look at your life style and what it affords you.

Ask yourself if there are things that you want in your life that you don't currently have time or money for?

Are there things that you have wanted for yourself since childhood that you have never allowed yourself?

Talk with your partner and figure out a way to give this to yourself. It will bring a deep sense of accomplishment and completion.

Make a life circle.

Decide how many slices you need to divide the circle into as you look at your life. Examples are your relationships, family, work, spiritual life, friends, personal time, and exercise. Be honest and divide it according to how you are *currently* spending your time. Once you have honestly looked at where you are now, make a circle and divide it the way you want to spend your time. This will help you budget time and finances, to bring more balance and happiness.

How does your money flow?

Are you spending within your means? Are you in the hole? If you are spending more than you make, look at ways to correct this imbalance. This is a dilemma that is encouraged by credit card companies. It allows you to create great mental and emotional stress.

By spending beyond your current financial means, you dig financial holes that are hard to climb out of. If you have a habit of overspending, you need to look deeply at how you overspend your energy and the inability to take energy in and build reserves.

Cut back on what you spend each day, week, and month.

This is one way to stop digging the hole deeper. Your peace of mind and the ability to build a lasting relationship depend on your ability to build financial stability. Stop the bad habits of overspending before they drive you to bankruptcy in both your financial and emotional life.

Build financial freedom.

It is never too late to begin living within your own means and begin to save money. Savings means financial security, independence, and the ability to begin to slow your life down. Once you reach this place in your life, you can slow the pace and begin to smell the roses.

Build a plan for retirement.

Many couples and individuals, have retirement plans that no longer work. Plans based solely on the stock market are no longer valid to produce the income needed to supplement retirement. Planning for retirement today takes thinking outside the box, using creativity and inner skills that you were born to uncover.

Dare to dream!

Dare to dream and build the inner strength to believe in yourself then follow through on your ideas. What is the difference between these two people: a person has a dream and follows an inner hunch to become a millionaire, the other person has a dream, and gets the same hunch but his "inner-critic" says it would be too difficult to create? Inner strength and discipline to believe that you can accomplish anything in life is born from the ability to focus on what you want and an inner determination to never give up.

Commit to your budget.

Once you have completed your Money Journal, determine what you need to be happy, and build a budget to support your chosen life style. Your budget allows you to plan your vacations, weekly or monthly dates, and your retirement. Dates don't need to be extravagant; sometimes simple dates have more meaning and create deeper intimacy. The important thing is to make your dates a priority and a habit.

To create a budget, take the money that you make each month, and figure out your expenses: rent, car payment, utility payments, and all monthly payments. Add in the expenses related to your job: gas, clothes, and supplies. These expenses will vary little and give you a basis for your expenditures each month. Look at the money you have left and negotiate how it is to be spent.

Make goals and follow a budget- it is fun and exciting.

Once the budget is created, create goals for three months, six months, one year and five years that support your budget, and vision. Once these goals are made, make a collage based on your goals and vision and add this to your "Heart Connections' Manual". (You will find the Heart Connections Manual instructions in chapter 10). Make index cards and put those on your bathroom mirror. For example you might have a goal to own a home in the next year. Write all the things you are looking for in that home. Jerry and I did this when we had given up hope of owning and finding a home in California. Start with how you feel in that home, where the home is located, size, price range, list all your dreams you are aware of. Be as specific as possible. The following examples may help you get started.

Index Card Example 1
Owning a Home in One Year

Date: By _____ 200_

I see myself in my new home. I feel very comfortable in this home; it is light and open, built of materials that are eco-friendly, and the colors are vibrant but soothing to my spirit. I feel a deep sense of gratitude for this home. I see my family and friends visiting and enjoying the loving environment. I see a space for plants, and a gray water system to reclaim the water to water our garden and indoor greenhouse. The house is built of materials that absorb the sun's warmth in the winter and repel heat in the summer. It is off the grid and has alternate energy systems including solar and hydro-electric. This home is a blessing to me, my community, and to the planet. It is easy to feel myself in this home, to see the home and my environment around my new home. I see herbs growing in and around my home, and a beautiful garden, with a gardener who assists us. The plants are happy, I am happy, and the environment around me is happy.

INDEX CARD EXAMPLE 2
A New Job

Date: By _____ 200_

I see myself in a career that feeds my spirit, challenges and expands my mind, and allows my emotions to be relaxed and calm. The people who are around me are supportive and like-minded. I feel a deep sense of gratitude for the doors that open for me to be of service to my community, my brothers and sisters, and to spirit. I see large sums of money in my bank account each month from this new career. I am calm, clear, and happy, and have endless amounts of energy to passionately give to this new career.

INDEX CARD EXAMPLE 3
A Growing Bank Account

Date: By _____ 200_

I see my bank account growing steadily each month. I see myself paying bills with a grateful heart. The money coming in is larger than the money that goes out. I give thanks to have this money to pay all my bills and have a larger and larger amount left over at the end of each month. I am grateful for my life, all the things that fill my environment, my car, my job, my family, and friends and home.

Sing a gratitude mantra

I sing a little song often-over and over in my mind. Thank you, Thank you, Thank you, Thank you, Thank you. As I sing I hold a vision of my bank account growing larger. I feel safe, secure and grateful.

Make index cards for whatever you want to create in your life. If you don't have a life partner, make a card to create your life partner. The thank you mantra song is simple and yet an effective way to create what you want in your life. Simply sing the song over and over in your mind as you hold a vision of what you want to attract. Hold a feeling of gratitude for having it in your life *now*.

Love's Secret number five
Vision for Love

Love one another, but make not a bond of love: Let it rather be a moving sea between the shores of your souls

-Kahlil Gibran

Destination Love without a Map

Judy longed for love; it was her deepest heart's desire. But she didn't have a vision of a loving relationship. Judy grew up as the youngest of nine children. Her parents were pretty burned out when she was born. She never received much attention, touch, or affection from her mom. As a matter of fact Judy had memories from her mom's womb of not being wanted. Her mom had thought that she was through menopause and could no longer get pregnant; she had not had a period for six months. Then came the big surprise; she was pregnant.

Judy made a decision that the world was not a safe place that she didn't deserve to be loved, and would never find love. How do you create a vision for a loving relationship when you haven't experienced love?

Love's Secret Number 5 is to create a vision for a relationship that incorporates all your dreams and inner desires. This vision focuses your intent and acts as your road map. In this chapter you will find exercises to help you fine tune your vision to create the relationship that you have searched for. You will find tools to keep you focused; connect to love, and practice intentional living.

Searching for Love with No Reference

Have you ever felt yourself craving something inside, like chocolate? Imagine that you have tasted chocolate, but for some reason you have suppressed the memory. You smell it and look at it and see others who love it and cherish it. But for some strange reason, you are afraid to try it. You find yourself dreaming about it, obsessing about it, looking at others who seem to be blessed by having it in their lives. But you can't break down and allow yourself to experience it.

Chocolate is everywhere on TV, at the checkout stand, you find it everywhere you turn. You search your mind but you can't figure out how you could be so obsessed with chocolate and yet terrified to give it a try.

A Taste of Euphoria

Finally you decide you have to try it out and you break down, euphoria fills your soul as you over indulge your senses. The next day you feel sick and depressed as suppressed memories begin to flood your awareness. Vague images fill your mind and haunt you, vows made as a child never to open yourself up to this experience again. The pain is too much, so you retreat back into the familiar comfort of your cloak of denial and shut down.

Love and Chocolate

Yes love and chocolate can bring euphoria in one moment and sink you to the very depths of your deepest, darkest pits the next. As you move through your fears and release the need for your cloak of denial, you can embrace the experience of love and chocolate. You can accept the euphoria and avoid the pit falls. Each experience must be embraced with balance, awareness, and clear intent to achieve the ultimate outcome.

A Vision for Love

Judy enrolled in a yoga and meditation class. She became aware of how her thoughts created an energy field around her body, and was the magnet that pulled in the experiences that she had on a day-to-day basis. Through her class Judy learned to focus her thoughts and energy on what she wanted.

Almost immediately she met someone. She found him attractive both on the outside and inside. The attraction was mutual. Finally, she had found the man of her dreams and was committed to creating a relationship based on love.

Role Models for Love

Neither Judy nor Larry had a vision of what they wanted to create, but had faith that they could build a vision. They asked for guidance from within to build a vision to act as a road map for creating a relationship filled with love. We met when they decided they needed help in creating their vision.

Dream Life Visioning

In our first session I decided to have them do an exercise called Dream Life Visioning. I gave them a blank sheet of paper and asked them to write about their lives without any self-imposed limits and inner judgments. They were to look at life as a blank slate without limitation. Anything they wanted or had secretly dreamed of, but denied themselves, was to be included. I encouraged them to write, draw, and dream, and put it on paper. They were to imagine their pen being magic and connected to all their dreams they had denied.

I guided them to move outside their usual box of limitations and tap into the limitless possibilities within. As they pulled their dreams from inside and got them on paper, they were to stay aware of their inner dialogue.

As they created their dream lives, they wrote down what their inner critic had to say. This gave me information I needed to help them in clearing their inner blocks to create their dream relationship.

Create Your Own Dream Life Vision

Follow the information above and create your own Dream Life Vision. Look at what you have written and what is included in your life. How do you envision your relationship? This is the basis of your Relationship Vision and will act as your road map to keep you focused on making love.

The Intentional Life

Judy and Larry were learning to build an intentional life and relationship in which they each felt empowered by their actions and choices. Through meditation, their hearts felt lighter than they had ever experienced. Yoga and meditation had become a tool to keep them focused and anchor their new life choices and habits.

Heart's Desires

Meditation and yoga had taught them how to access their inner wisdom. This gave them a mutual tool for connecting to their heart to access their heart's desires. They uncovered their hidden desires, and found joy in giving and receiving them. Committing to a relationship in which both partners feel their hearts' desire is being fulfilled is easy. Practicing giving and receiving their desires was an anchoring tool for love and built deeper bonds of trust.

Sharing My Goals and Dreams

In searching my own heart for my vision for my relationship, I discovered I wanted someone who I felt equal to. I wanted someone who could share my ideas and dreams. In order to feel safe to share this deep longing, I needed my partner to be a good listener. It didn't matter if he always agreed with me. What mattered most was that he listened to my ideas. Being present with someone and hearing what they need to verbalize establishes trust and creates fertile ground for intimacy.

Love Anchors Trust through Listening

Sometimes my partner will play devil's advocate, which helps me determine how committed I am to my idea. I always appreciate his listening and giving feedback, because I know his feedback is heartfelt and honest. In order to invite my partner's honest opinion I have to allow him to disagree with my ideas and not feel threatened or rejected. I have learned to feel comfortable within myself to be challenged by different view points, which establishes deeper trust for my partner to voice his honest opinion.

To establish deep intimacy you must become comfortable with your partner's sharing his or her opinion without agreeing with you. As you sacrifice your need to be right and agreed with, you create new pathways of trust and communication.

A Soul Connection

As I looked deeply within for my vision, I discovered I wanted someone to share my spirituality. I wanted to pray and meditate together and create goals. These goals were both spiritual and life goals. We have found our passion in life and have found an ability to share it. Both of us feel very passionate about many things: our spiritual lives, art, writing, health, gardening, and earth stewardship. What a wonderful gift it is to look deeply within, find your passion, and share it with your life partner.

Secrets for Making Love

⚫ Give up the addiction to the feeling of being in love and commit to building authentic love.

⚫ Focus your energy on thoughts that build love.

⚫ Make love and your partnership a priority, daily.

⚫ Practice the attitude of excitement and trust, and drown out fear of rejection and abandonment.

⚫ When you give what you want to receive you gift yourself the benefit of giving and receiving love.

⚫ Excitement is as contagious as depression but feels much better.

⚫ A hug a day given from a pure heart without expectation; is a gift of joy and will make your heart glow.

Use EFT To Open Your Heart To Love.

The words and phrases are based on beliefs that may have surfaced as you created your Dream Life Vision. Listen closely as you tap, and find hidden beliefs and emotions. As you practice EFT, notice your inner reactions and find you own specific beliefs. Insert your issues as they come to the surface to be healed.

The more you practice EFT, the more comfortable you will become. You will be guided from inside to the words and phrases to use. Before you begin, test yourself and find your inner level of fear of opening your heart to experience love. Measure your fear on a scale of 0-10. How much fear do you have of opening your heart to love? While asking yourself the same questions hold a picture in your mind of a scene that brings up fear of love. This can be a break-up from someone that you loved and trusted or a scene from your childhood where you felt denied love.

☾ Begin by tapping on the top of the center of your head. Repeat as you tap, "Even though I may have a belief that I don't deserve love, still I choose to deeply and completely love and accept myself."

☾ Tap on the area between your eyebrows, at the inside edge of each eyebrow, above the bridge of your nose. Repeat as you tap, "Even though I have never experienced love and may have made a decision as a little (girl or boy) that I don't deserve love, still I choose to deeply and completely love and accept myself."

79

❦ **Tap on the outside corner of each eye. Repeat as you tap,** "This old fear of love and being hurt, while longing for love, I created this fear in my childhood and it still causes me to push love away. Still I choose to deeply and completely love and accept myself."

❦ **Tap on the outside corner of each nostril. Repeat as you tap,** "These decisions I made as a little (girl or boy) based on the writing on my walls and my past experiences as a child. This is just an old story written to create my life journey, and create my life lessons. Still I choose to deeply and completely love and accept myself."

❦ **Tap on the center of the upper lip just below your nose. Repeat as you tap,** "These old fears of love connected to pain and craving love were old habits created by a little (girl or boy) who longed to be loved and acknowledged. Just old conditioning, not who I am, I am not my conditioning from my parents or my environment; I am more than my conditioning and reactions. I can take my power back from my addiction to pain and my longing for love and choose to create a new feeling of being safe and reconnect love to feeling good. Still I choose to deeply and completely love and accept myself."

❦ **Tap on the center of the chin just below the lower lip. Repeat as you tap,** "Even though I may have made a vow to myself that I would never allow myself to be vulnerable and open my heart to love. Still I choose to deeply and completely love and accept myself."

☾ **Tap on the top of the chest at the inside of each clavicle or chest bone, just below your chin where your neck meets your chest. Repeat as you tap,** "Even though I long to feel love and dream of creating a loving relationship, I am terrified of being hurt, if I open my heart.   This old pattern of craving love and being terrified of love is a pattern that seems to repeat and have control over me. Still I deeply and completely love and accept myself."

☾ **Tap just below your underarm in the armpit area in line with the nipple. Repeat as you tap,** "Even though I have beaten myself up with this old belief and pattern, still I deeply and completely love and accept myself and choose to release the fear of opening my heart to experience love.   I give myself permission to feel safe to create new patterns and habits of being open to love."

After completing this EFT tapping session check inside again and test with the same scale of 0-10. Hold a scene in your mind of being rejected by love. How much fear do you have of opening your heart to love? Keep working either alone or with your mate to bring the score to zero.

Love's Secret for Fine Tuning Your Vision

☾ Focus on love and create a picture in your mind of a loving supportive relationship.

☾ Write down everything you want to receive from your relationship.

🍂 See your relationship providing a safe place to communicate your deepest desires.

🍂 See your mate as someone you can dream with and then put the goals into action to create your dreams.

🍂 See your mate as someone who brightens your day each morning and gives comfort as each day ends.

Give your hearts, but not into each others keeping

-Kahlil Gibran

Interdependence Vision

I hope you now have a better understanding of where you are in your relationship and what you want to create. Take some time individually to write a vision from your heart that makes you feel good.

Come together and discuss your visions. Listen to each other with your heart open and negotiate a unified vision that will meet the needs of each partner. If you run into differences that you are unable to reconcile, seek out a relationship coach, counselor, or minister you both trust.

Your vision of being in love many times gets stuck in trying to recreate passion felt at an immature stage of past relationships. This can become an addiction to a feeling of being in love and begin a quest to recreate relationships over and over.

This is the path of a passion junkie. To maintain the euphoric high, longer than one or two years; a revolving door of new relationships must be pursued. If this pattern is not stopped, fear of intimacy becomes stronger than the need for intimacy.

Do not confuse these relationships with a vision for long-term partnerships. Focusing only on passion does not create a loving space for deeper growth and development.

A Vision for Love Template

Our partnership provides a safe place to share any feelings and dreams. We are supportive of each other's individual dreams and goals. Some of the goals and dreams are mutual.

We set aside uninterrupted time for heart expressions at least weekly, and stay current with our emotions.   Each heart expressions session begins with the intent to hold each other's heart in our hands gently, and stay in touch with our love, as we listen quietly.

We each remain present and listen attentively with our hearts open, and offer support to each other. After we feel heard, we switch roles and welcome honest feedback. Our hearts remain open and connected to our love as we allow disagreement and resist any old urges to react by feeling rejected and shut down.

Time for introspection and taking inventory of our thoughts, habits, and patterns, are part of our mutual life choices. We choose to develop healthy habits for being in relationship and practice being pro-active in life.

Habits and patterns not connected to joy and happiness are eliminated. We spend time and energy in developing habits that deepen our love and passion, and expand joy.

My partner and I find ways to communicate our passion, deepen our heart-connection, and have fun in our relationship.

We each have a connection to the Divine and make time for that individually and as a couple.

We continue to learn new ways to laugh and play, and include play time in our schedule. Each of us supports the other in our growth and in expressing our individual creativity.

Our commitment to our love and relationship builds trust and allows us to feel safe to share our deep desires.

Our relationship has priority over all individuals, activities, and material possessions in our life.

We are each committed to our own individual exercise routines, and take good care of our mental, emotional, and spiritual bodies.

Intimate activities are a priority, such as love-making, cuddling, and being present for each other without interruption. To support these activities we create time within our schedule for dates and continue the habit of courting.

By practicing excitement and trust for each other and our partnership, we drown out fear and deepen our love.

We stay committed to our own happiness and to our partner's happiness.

We practice the attitude of gratitude for our life, love, joy, passion, expanding awareness, and growth. We take time each day to give thanks for each other and our love. We develop a grateful heart.

Love's Secret number six
Love Habits

*D*on't wait for someone else to create your dream life-focus
your energy and create your dreams today!

-ANNIE LAWRENCE

Build a Strong Foundation for Love

Carol and Dan were in a state of euphoria. They had
planned this wedding for four years and tomorrow was
their day. Clothes were carefully packed and reservations
made for their honeymoon. Carol's first dream for her
wedding occurred more than ten years ago, when she was
fourteen. Since that time, she had carefully planned each
detail in her mind. She and Dan had spent hour's online
researching details of their honeymoon destination and
what it offered. They didn't want to miss out on one
moment's pleasure.

Love's Secret Number 6 is to develop love habits that support your vision and provide a strong foundation for your
relationship. In this chapter you will find a plan for the
most important trip of your life, your life partnership.

Wedding Bell Blues

Imagine you're embarking on a trip. This trip may last for the rest of your life; you hope your dreams will come true. You plan a big public exhibition to celebrate your trip. You get caught up in the planning and spend all your time and money, and you have no time to prepare yourself for the journey. The celebration is your total focus; dreaming and obsessing about it every moment of each day.

You trust that the journey will take care of itself. You spare no expense for the celebration. Planning it gets out of control and you go way over budget. You spend money you don't have and put it on your credit card. The joy of the celebration gets lost in the complications of what's expected from your friends and family. The performance of the celebration comes and goes and everything is a blur.

Your journey begins without any preparation, and you find yourself in foreign territory without skills. Everything in your life is now different. You thought you wanted to take this journey but now you find yourself miserable and in debt.

Preparing for the Love Journey

Six months after their marriage, Carol is feeling so depressed and blue she can hardly drag herself out of bed each morning. Dan is wondering what happened to the

happy young woman who used to be his friend and com-
panion. Their days had been spent dreaming about their
married life together. Their life now doesn't resemble
their dreams. Planning the wedding had been their focus,
now it seems as though they don't have anything in common. All their dreams seem to have faded into feelings of
hopelessness and despair.

They took it for granted that once they got married,
it would just happen and that they would continue to be
happy together. They wished they would have known
that they needed new skills in order to build a happy
married life.

Love Takes the Wrong Turn

Dan sought help, and when they entered my office,
the couple looked lost and hopeless. We spent some time
weeding out the habits that had them caught in pain.
Once the pain was cleared, Dan and Carol could feel the
love that had drawn them together in the beginning.

Carol and Dan's plan to build love habits included
monthly coaching sessions to keep them focused on their
vision. Each month we reviewed their progress with
establishing their love habits. These habits included
weekly "heart-expression" sessions. Expressing their
emotions on a weekly basis kept them current and established a deeper heart connection.

Carol and Dan learned how to stay connected with

their love and express disagreements. Sometimes they had to agree to disagree with each other and choose not to feel rejected. Before their coaching, they had reacted to disagreements by distancing and shutting down.

After falling into their deep, dark hole of pain and despair, Carol wished they would have learned the skills before they married. Her comfortable cloud of denial had her blissfully assuming that married life with Dan would evolve like in the TV show *Leave It To Beaver* and that they would live happily ever after.

With their vision in hand to act as a road map, and armed with tools for communicating from their hearts, they felt confident of success in their marriage. They now understood where they would go if they continued down the road of reaction to old habits. They were committed to invest the time and discipline to develop habits that supported love and their vision.

Habits for Love

Below you will find some of most effective love habits gathered from Jerry and my moments together, and what has worked most effectively with our clients.

☾ Start each day with gratitude; by thinking of all the things you have in your life for which you are grateful. Next, visualize your day and see the very best outcome. Start your visualization by holding a picture of your vision for your relationship. Feel the love you have in your heart for your mate, and see that feeling of love as a pink cocoon surrounding him or her.

☾ Throughout your day, when you think of your mate, send a feeling of love to him or her. See them with a smile on their face, and focus on your heart. Each time you think of your mate train yourself to think about something that you love about them: their smile, their laugh, the warm cozy feeling when they hug you, anything they do that feels special to you. Each time you practice this love habit you anchor and expand your love.

☾ Leave your mate love notes somewhere that will surprise them. Your love note can be left in a brief case, on a mirror, or on a steering wheel. Be creative.

☾ Make a list of what you love about your mate and look at the list at least once a day; focus your love to them.

☾ Make a list of the things you want to receive from your partner. Give at least one thing from your partner's list to him or her each day. This can be as simple as a hug when you are focused on love.

☾ Heart expression sessions are scheduled each week, to stay current with your emotions. In this session share from your heart; be sure not to make it a dumping session. Speak in terms of "I" and share what you are feeling. Ask for what you would like to receive. Ask without expectation of outcome.

During this session learn to share any unresolved feelings and stay current with your emotions. Don't continue habits of holding on to resentment or anger. Learn to release and let go.

When you share in your "heart expression" sessions, share first what you feel, then share what you want. Keep focused on creating a deeper bond and stay connected to your love. For instance rather than saying, "You make me angry when you go out with your friends and don't call me." Instead say, "I feel angry and hurt when you go out and don't call. What I would like is if you call me and let me know where you are, so I can feel safe to keep my heart open." "When I feel hurt at your lack of communication, it makes me want to shut down and push you away." What ever you are feeling, resolve your feelings and stay current.

Resolve all conflicts before bed. Make it a rule never to take arguments to bed. Make your bed a special "sacred space" for love. And never go to bed with unresolved conflict. When you hit an area where you can't reach an agreement, agree to disagree for the moment. Seek help to find a resolution.

When you have areas of unresolved conflict, the quicker you get help, the better. The longer you allow the conflict, the more damage and the greater the distance that comes between you and your love.

Avoid angry words - they destroy love. Once words are said it puts imprints on the mind and the heart. For each angry word it takes 100 kind loving words to rebuild a bridge to the heart and re-establish trust.

Love's Garden

Relationships are like a garden; you must plant seeds of love and kindness daily and nurture it with care to keep it flourishing.

Weed old beliefs, patterns, and survival skills; they create fear, anger, resentment, and guilt, and smother your ability to keep your heart open.

Harvest rewards of commitment through growth and deepening your bond of love.

Buried in deep fertile grounds of divine union are the keys to authentic love. That union requires a commitment to personal growth and healing.

Destructive weeds of old habits will resurface to cause toxic reactions, until you learn to be present and react with love.

Like a neglected garden that becomes overgrown with weeds, your mind and relationship require constant presence to make choices that enhance love, moment to moment.

-ANNIE LAWRENCE

When you become over-emotional about a current life event, be assured: you are touching a wound from the past.

Stay committed to find and remove patterns that plague your life with chaos, fear, and unhappiness. Change your reaction. At times you may become confused and want to go back to what felt normal or familiar. Keep practicing your new love habits. Love habits will become automatic, just like the old habits were, and it will feel better once you have moved through the fear of change.

When situations push buttons wired to painful toxic emotions, the mind feels like a maze of twists and turns. Stay present and keep making decisions based in love. The fear of change will pass! Love emotions, like joy and happiness, flood your body with chemicals that make your life worth living. Joyful happy emotions are worth the effort to establish. Stay on track and keep unraveling your inner web of emotions and patterns.

Remember: Old decisions, thoughts, and patterns, are intertwined with your adult life and current events.

Find your self-defeating habits and patterns that cause pain, and make new choices. Don't be a puppet with your strings being pulled by outdated programming.

Evelyn's Story

Evelyn felt like a puppet on a string, with someone or

something pulling her strings without permission. Her emotions were always on the surface just waiting for the right life situation to bring them out. She felt victimized by life, her work, and all her relationships, past and present. Evelyn found herself on a merciless merry-go-round without a clue of how to get off. Often, she wondered why her life was always prone to disaster, while others around her led a "charmed life."

She had been praying for relief from her plight when she stumbled on a flyer for a free introductory evening at our clinic. Evelyn was desperate enough to try anything especially if it was free. Arriving home early that evening, she was shaking with excitement, and anxious to receive any help offered.

That night as Evelyn entered our small clinic, I remember how anxious she seemed for help. I explained the rules of the mind and how the mind and emotions work. She seemed to hang onto each word and had interesting questions which opened the group for discussion.

Evelyn Seeks Help

She shared that her life had been plagued with pain and depression, and that she wanted to understand her mind so that she might change her reactions. Evelyn listened intently but found it hard to grasp the new concepts. Did she carry her mom's voice around in her head constantly? "No, this can't be true," she gasped. "I hate her and I would never allow her to exist in my head. I left home at age sixteen and have never looked back and never had any desire to return for a visit."

Evelyn thought about the voice she heard constantly, which judged every move. It was the critical voice of her mother. Evelyn had grown up the second child with an older brother. Her brother had taken over her father's position and could do no wrong in her mother's eyes. Evelyn, had become a constant doormat for anger and resentment her mother felt for being abandoned. Never good enough, never able to do enough to win her mother's love, Evelyn gave up and left.

She got a job at a local McDonald's, and found a live-in situation with an older woman who needed help. She studied and took her GED test and received her high school diploma. At seventeen, she began college, and completed her basic courses. Although gruff and armored with a tough exterior, the older woman was genuine and trustworthy. She never showed much affection or gave Evelyn much acknowledgement, but she was the most positive influence in her life. And she soon won Evelyn's heart and became the grandmother she had always wanted. Grandma Bessie had given Evelyn a safe place to live, off the streets.

Attempt to Find Love

The first relationship Evelyn had was when she was

eighteen. Before she met John, she had never allowed herself to trust anyone. This was her first failed attempt to experience love. John was a real user and manipulator. He liked the idea that Evelyn was a virgin and courted her very heavily, until finally she gave in. This short-lived relationship drove the nail deeper into Evelyn's heart. The lack of love and respect from John convinced her even more that she was ugly, dirty, and did not deserve to be loved. John dumped her after only two short weeks.

Evelyn had been "saving" herself for the right person, and because John pursued her so strongly, she thought that he was her prince. This failed attempt at love threw her deeply into a depression. She decided she would never trust anyone again, especially a man.

Evelyn Feels Hopeless

Shortly after this heart-breaking relationship Grandma Bessie became very ill. After a month in a coma and several strokes, Bessie passed away. Evelyn was devastated. She had no one to turn to and no longer had a place to live. Evelyn wandered downtown after the memorial service for Bessie. She didn't know where to turn, but didn't want to be alone. A small Coffee-Book shop caught her eye and she decided to go in. It felt good not to be alone.

A young girl about her age walked up to her table and asked if she could sit down. They began to talk about their lives and found that they had a lot in common. Joan, her new friend, had just moved to the area and felt very alone. She was looking to find a roommate to help with her expenses, but was afraid because she didn't know anyone. They were both delighted and felt that their prayers had led them to meet. They agreed upon rental terms and made arrangements for Evelyn to spend the night, and then move her things in the next day.

Searching Inside for Hidden Answers

In our hypnotherapy session, I explained that we all have a conscious mind and a subconscious mind, and each plays a role in how we live our lives. The two parts of the mind are two very different control centers for our body, mind, and emotions. The conscious mind is in control when we are awake, making decisions and continuously controlling body functions. The unconscious mind controls our thoughts and unconscious mind chatter and assists the conscious mind to make decisions.

The unconscious mind is like a sleeping giant, who is constantly gathering and storing information, even without our permission or awareness. At a moment's notice, the conscious mind reaches into the unconscious mind for past experiences and makes a snap judgment for today's events. Faster that you can blink your eye, the two centers check for past experiences. A decision is made, without awareness of the process to reach the decision.

Once a decision is stored in the subconscious mind, it remains there until we consciously retrieve it, and replace it with a new decision.

Evelyn began to wonder what she had buried in her subconscious. As she looked back, her life seemed like a horror story but how did she as a child interpret it. What was in her mind that had caused her to make a decision to trust John? Why would she open her heart to someone so undeserving?

I explained that sometimes we draw our deepest fears to us. Evelyn felt confused and lost in the maze built by her mind. She decided to face her fears and find her buried answers; she picked up the phone and made an appointment for a private hypnotherapy session.

Never Felt Love-Afraid to Feel Love

Evelyn explained that she wanted to be in love and get married, but was terrified to trust again. She explained that she had never felt love, so she was confused about how to recognize the right person when he came into her life.

I explained that she needed to forgive and release the past, before she could be free to move forward. I also explained that she needed to learn to love herself before she could share that love.

Evelyn's Regression

Scared and excited at the same time, Evelyn prepared to relax as I guided her into the deep recesses of her mind.

Her journey inside her mind went back to the time she was in her mother's womb. Her mother was sobbing and pleading with Evelyn's father to stay and not leave. It seems that her mother was pregnant by another man, not her husband. From that moment forward, Evelyn had a deep core belief that she didn't deserve to be born. Buried in guilt and deep shame, she had never accessed the logical reason. Only one other time had she felt such deep guilt and shame: when John dumped her.

Evelyn Forgives

I guided Evelyn to forgive her mother for the guilt imposed on her. Realizing why she felt deep shame and guilt, Evelyn was able to change this deep core belief. She chose to forgive herself and her mother, and learned to love herself.

Evelyn now saw how her relationship with John had brought deeply-engrained feelings of guilt and shame to the surface to be healed. Before surfacing her hidden memories, she had not been able to forgive herself or John. I explained how holding on to anger or resentment was like drinking poison daily and hoping the people who hurt you would die.

Evelyn had battled a deep depression throughout her young life. After our hypnotherapy session, she felt a big weight was lifted from her shoulders.

Evelyn Finds Hope

For the first time in her life, Evelyn began to feel hope for a happy life. She had a roommate who felt like a sister she had never had. Once Evelyn had forgiven her mother, herself, her unknown father, and John, new doors began to open. She received a job promotion, something that she had been praying for since she took the position. Two weeks later, she bumped into someone who she had admired at work and he asked her out.   She was feeling so happy, she began to feel afraid, but then she realized that it was just change.

Monitoring her self-talk and inner feelings had been something that she was learning in our hypnotherapy group. She quickly assured herself that she was safe, and deserved to be happy. She welcomed all the good life had to offer.

When you have been stuck in pain all your life, no matter how miserable, moving away from that misery will bring up fear. In order to release the fear, you must feel the fear and acknowledge it, but continue to make choices that support happiness.

Love's Secret by Evelyn

☾ As you develop new patterns of thought and establish new love habits it will bring up fear.

☾ Feel your fear by confronting it with awareness, rather than denying or ignoring it. As you feel it continue making healthy choices. Hold a picture in your mind of yourself with a smile. "Love Habits" won't feel comfortable in the beginning. Fear activates your survival response, but you can choose to change your response.

☾ Old patterns are familiar and seem comfortable even though they contain pain. Habits are comfortable only because they are familiar and all you have ever experienced. Compare this to an old pair of worn sneakers, that have worn heels and soles that don't serve your posture, but feel comfy and familiar. When you try on a new pair of shoes, your feet might rebel, even though you love the new pair. Just like your feet, you will adapt and love the fit and comfort of new habits.

☾ Love may be connected to pain, shame, and guilt through your nerve pathways. Subconsciously, Evelyn had wired love to pain, shame, and guilt, and she was recreating the feeling of longing for love and feeling rejected. Subconscious patterns repeat until the pattern is cleared and new pathways are made that connect love to healthy feelings.

☾ Stop reacting to old patterns and build new nerve pathways to images of love in your mind and cellular structure. Deep patterns like Evelyn's may require professional help to retrieve core issue and resolve toxic automatic reactions to life.

Contemplating the Story

☾ What touched your heart? What pushed a button in you?

☾ What is the predominate emotion you are feeling?

☾ Which part did you relate to?

☾ Look back at past relationships. Who was the dominant personality?

EFT for Releasing Struggle

What personality in your childhood is most similar? A father or mother who was a workaholic, or addicted to drugs, or alcohol? Anyone who was emotionally abusive, and not emotionally available?

Use EFT to release the fear of being happy. Check in to see if you might have an addiction to struggle. On a scale of 0-10, do you fear having a happy, successful life? Hold a picture in your mind in which you might have been happy and then noticed that you sabotaged yourself.

☾ **Begin by tapping on the top of the center of your head. Repeat as you tap,** "Even though I may

have a belief that I don't deserve to be happy and succeed, still I choose to deeply and completely love and
accept myself."

⬩ **Tap on the area between your eyebrows, at the
inside edge of each eyebrow, above the bridge of
your nose. Repeat as you tap,** "Even though I have
never experienced long term happiness and sustained
success and may have made a decision as a little(girl or
boy) that life is a struggle, still I choose to deeply and
completely love and accept myself."

⬩ **Tap on the outside corner of each eye. Repeat as
you tap,** "This old fear of success and being rejected, but
longing for success and happiness, decisions made in my
childhood and cause me to push love away.   Still I choose
to deeply and completely love and accept myself."

⬩ **Tap on the outside corner of each nostril. Repeat
as you tap,** "These decisions I made as a little (girl or
boy) based on the writing on my walls and my past experiences as a child, are just old stories written to create my
life journey and my life lessons. Still I choose to deeply
and completely love and accept myself."

⬩ **Tap on the center of the upper lip just below
your nose. Repeat as you tap,** "These old fears of
being happy and being rejected by family and friends are
just an old fear created by a little (girl or boy) who longed

to be loved and acknowledged. I can take my power back from my addiction to struggle and longing for success. I choose to create a new feeling of being safe, and reconnect success to feeling good. Still I choose to deeply and completely love and accept myself."

☾ **Tap on the center of the chin just below the lower lip. Repeat as you tap,** "Even though I may have made a vow that I would never allow myself to be successful and happy and feel the jealousy of friends and family. Still I choose to deeply and completely love and accept myself."

☾ **Tap on the top of the chest at the inside of each clavicle or chest bone just below your chin where your neck meets your chest. Repeat as you tap,** "Even though I long to feel happy and successful and long to create my dream life, I am terrified of being hurt, if I dream and fail. This old pattern of craving success, and being terrified of success and failure at the same time, is a pattern that seems to repeat and have control over me. Still I deeply and completely love and accept myself."

☾ **Tap just below your underarm in the armpit area in line with the nipple. Repeat as you tap,** "Even though I have beaten myself up with this old belief and pattern, still I deeply and completely love and accept myself and choose to release the fear of opening my heart to experience love and success. I give myself permission to feel safe to create love and success now.

After completing this EFT tapping session check inside yourself and test with the scale of 0-10. Hold a scene in your mind of being successful. Notice your feelings. How much fear of success do you feel? Do you still fear being rejected if you succeed? Now hold a scene in your mind of failure how much fear do you have? Keep working either alone or with your mate to bring both feelings scores down to zero.

The Secret for Choosing Love

☾ Make love your priority.

☾ Practice the attitude of gratitude and create a grateful heart and recommit to your relationship daily.

☾ Hurtful Words said in Anger, Scar the Heart for a Life-Time.

☾ Focus your thoughts on love-energy flows where you thoughts focus.

☾ Direct your energy on thoughts that build trust and love.

Love's Secret number seven
Create A Safe Place

It is not how much we do, but how much love we put in the doing. It is not how much we give, but how much love we put in the giving.

-MOTHER TERESA

Learning to Feel Safe

Karen had never felt safe, and doesn't know how to feel safe to open her heart to love. Her new relationship is young and she can hardly breathe. Terrified that the love she feels will vanish before her eyes. She holds on to her breath trying to freeze her feelings of euphoric bliss.

Boundaries

Love's Secret Number 7 is learning to feel safe and to trust. Commit to a partnership, remove the beliefs that push love away, and co-create a vision for your map. Then you are able to create a space for deep intimacy. This means creating interdependence rather than the co-dependent model of relationship. Trust is an essential ingredient for both intimacy and interdependence. Each partner needs to have a good balance of time alone, outside friendships and interests, extended family, and good career boundaries.

Boundaries are the most difficult issue to address if your role models were co-dependent. For you, then, the word boundary has meanings of property lines or state borders.

When you are fully engaged with your own life, you bring a sense of wholeness to the relationship. Otherwise, you are continually drawing energy from the relationship to fill your needs, rather than sharing energy from a sense of being complete and healthy already.

Freedom Becomes a Bond

Glowing with euphoric bliss, Karen appeared to be walking on a cloud as she entered my office. The bliss hid her deep terror of reactivating past toxic relationship habits. As she settled in for her first coaching session, she said she had a deep fear of failure. EFT released some of those fears and by the end of the first session, she felt hope and began to feel safe to relax.

When you feel complete as you enter a partnership, freedom becomes a bond for the relationship. Sharing love from a sense of wholeness creates freedom to breathe and be one's self. This freedom includes healthy boundaries and commitment. It creates the space to deepen trust. Each partner feels safe to grow and express deeper levels of who they are.

Interdependence creates a good foundation for a deep spiritual connection and creates a safe space to evolve to the highest level. A partnership built on love and mutual trust provides the support of a like-minded soul. This supportive relationship serves to mirror your good personality traits and heal your shadow traits. You become a loving reflection of your partner, and, through this reflection, support each other to complete work you came together to do.

Co-Dependent Behavior Patterns

Karen had never taken time to think about how she reacted to life. Living on auto-pilot gave her a sense of comfort. Her fog of denial assured her that her next relationship would be different.

The deep soul connection she felt with her new partner had her hoping this could be "Mister Right." She felt driven to give it her best shot and get it right this time. In the past she gave everything including her heart and became consumed by her mate. She felt a deep "inner drive to win his love." In the end, her over-giving and lack of respect for herself pushed her "intended" away.

Toxic habits in a co-dependent relationship sabotage intimacy and trust. Over-giving and manipulation through giving in order to receive what you crave, destroys intimacy and usually ends in divorce. Set clear boundaries in your relationships by being clear about what you want. Ask for what you want in gentle, non-threatening, non-demanding ways. When you clearly ask without being upset by the outcome, you are more likely to get your needs met.

Set Boundaries

Karen had been caught in a pattern of longing and seeking love. She had never moved beyond this dance into real intimacy. Her pain and her deep desire to make love last, motivated her to seek help. We removed layers of denial and pain, and helped her to recognize her worth and gain self-esteem.

She developed habits of being happy and giving to herself the things she enjoyed. This allowed her to give for the joy of giving, without expectations. In the past she had addictively been an over-giver. Her giving came from a need to receive and had agendas attached.

She learned that by giving herself love and respect, she found her "mate" gave her love and respect as well.

Safe Space for Intimacy

Sharing love from a sense of wholeness, without expectation of return, creates freedom to breathe and be oneself within a relationship.

A partnership built on love and mutual trust, offers support from a like-minded soul who recognizes and mirrors your good qualities and helps you to grow beyond your challenges.

Release agendas and hidden needs so that trust and freedom becomes a bond for your relationship.

Wedding Plans Announced

Karen had been receiving coaching sessions for six months. I had encouraged her to take it slow and build a good, strong foundation. Love habits were a part of a daily routine with her new love. She was ecstatic when she arrived with a new ring on her finger and announced her wedding date.

"A hug, given without expectation, makes your heart glow, and creates a safe place for love!"

-ANNIE LAWRENCE

Fred Arrives Feeling Hopeless

When Fred walked into my office, his face was almost void of emotion. His eyes looked sad and tears rolled down his cheek as he shared his story.

Fred met Alice when he was in his early thirties. He had not been in a relationship more than one year. He longed to settle down, get married, and start a family. But at the end of a year, all the women he dated ended up looking and feeling the same. After one year, he explained, they all start to feel trapped. Passion began to fade and the women began to act just like his mom.

Fred never felt accepted and acknowledged by his mom. His mom was preoccupied with two jobs struggling to make the rent and pay the bills.

In our sessions Fred discovered what had led him to be an overachiever. He had spent his time as a boy, struggling to win his moms love and be accepted and acknowledged. In his relationships, Fred gave a lot to his women: flowers, gifts, and lots of compliments. He wanted so badly to win their love; he lost himself in pursuing love and acknowledgement. He never felt safe to be himself.

Totally immersed in his pursuit, he gave up all outside friendships or interests. The pursuit of love consumed Fred's life and was an endless loop of frustration and bitter endings. He found him self yo-yoing in ecstasy of new love and deep depression, as the relationships ended.

Recreating Rejection

Alice was his first attempt to make a deeper commitment. He felt his time clock running out. He wanted to find his life partner and create the family of his dreams. Alice was perfect, she was beautiful, funny, and they had many common interests.

Fred found himself noticing little things that bothered him, as the one-year anniversary rolled around. He wanted to spend more time together. Alice had her own life which included friends and she was very involved with her church. He didn't want to spend time with her church activities, and felt completely left out.

He began to make demands that she give up some of her activities and spend more time with him. He liked to stay home and watch a movie or hang out. Alice wasn't about to give up her friends or church. As Fred made his demands she became even more preoccupied and distant. This pushed a deep button for Fred; he felt abandoned, unacknowledged, unloved, and unappreciated.

Healing Denial and Hurt

Fred was beside himself, he felt like this could be his last chance. He was afraid that Alice had already made a decision that her life was more important than their relationship. He felt a hopeless feeling creeping back in again, and he felt driven to shut down and pull away. In our session, we decided to invite Alice and confront the situation before love was lost.

Fred had never slowed down between relationships long enough to see his patterns in his self-created hell. He didn't realize that Alice was the perfect person to assist him in healing his deep wounds from childhood. He knew he needed help but he didn't understand why he felt so much pain.

Past Hurt Created Distance

Alice shared her feelings and explained that she felt

controlled as a child, especially by her father. She told us that love was important to her but she needed her independence. It was very important to her. As a child, she was not allowed to have friends of her own, or to pursue her own interests.

As an adult, freedom had become as important to her as being in a relationship. Her friends and her extra activities were a joyful part of life. She would not consider giving them up. She loved to be busy and found it hard to relax and just hang out with Fred.

The more Fred pulled at her the more she wanted to push him away. She wanted to commit to a relationship and have a family. But a relationship would include her friends, and allow her independence. Even though she wanted a family, she was beginning to think it wasn't meant to be.

She felt that Fred was trying to control her and began to see him looking very similar to her father. She had been praying for the perfect relationship; she wanted to settle down and have the family she had dreamed of. This pattern had become a common thread in her trail of broken relationships. Alice had kept herself busy with friends, work, church, and unsatisfying relationships and never slowed down to figure out her painful patterns.

Pursuit of Love and Pushing Love Away

Alice and Fred were at a pivotal point in their relationship. They needed to recognize their patterns brought from childhood, or stay stuck pushing love away.

The magnetic pull bringing them together was their wounds created in their childhoods. They had to recognize this and commit to healing, or they would push love away again, and continue an endless search for the "perfect partner."

They were at a stalemate, and caught in pain. Through EFT sessions we removed heavy layers of pain and got their love back. Neither wanted to stay caught in the agony of their past love dance.

"And ever has it been that love knows not its own depth until the hour of separation."

-KAHLIL GIBRAN

Alice and Fred decided to create a different ending. Motivated by their internal clocks, they decided to own their hurt, and commit to their individual healing. They wanted to move forward and create a lasting partnership and family.

As a couple, they learned to appreciate their differences, and negotiate their individual needs. They learned to listen and communicate from their heart.

Making Love a Reality

Our coaching sessions trained them to communicate and negotiate their differences. Alice and Fred discovered that they had a deep love and appreciation for each other.

By practicing awareness, they learned to break the addiction to their destructive patterns and habits and make new choices. They discovered new ways to be happy within; together they began to create a relationship supporting positive emotions and happiness.

Tired of the "dating game" and the pursuit of love, they made a commitment to go to the next level and create the love they longed for. Alice and Fred were committed to create a life full of joy and to make love last.

Love's Secrets by Alice and Fred

⟐ To build love, communicate from your heart and use words that build trust and support love.

⟐ Passive-aggressive actions like putting someone else down in order to feel better, is a subtle habit that destroys love and trust. Awareness can assist in choosing new actions and reactions. Many times this may have happened to you and you may have made a vow to never do this to others. Then you catch yourself reacting automatically. You get angry with yourself, and create a vicious cycle of rejecting others and then rejecting yourself. This pattern often has a tight grip and may require a professional to assist with dismantling your addictive reaction to life.

⟐ No matter what your situation in childhood, you have

wounds to be healed and the perfect clinic to heal these wounds is a conscious, loving relationship. Stay committed and keep growing.

⟐ Act from awareness, and liberate yourself from toxic emotions and a flood of toxic chemicals to your nervous system and cells.

Inventory and journaling

Write in your journal in your peaceful quiet place. Light a candle and take some time to practice deep breathing. Once you are in touch with your inner wisdom. Say the affirmations and write your response.

⟐ I respect my mate and know what makes her or him happy. I enjoy giving the things they love without expectation.

⟐ I know what makes me happy and what I want from life and from my mate.

⟐ The things that I want most from my mate are easy to ask for, and I never make demands or have hidden agendas.

⟐ I make time in my daily and weekly routine for _____ just because this makes me happy.

⟐ I value and enjoy my alone time and make time for it daily and weekly.

⟐ I have an outside support system of friends. I value and make time for them in my life.

❦ I know my self, my inner dreams and desires. I have personal goals as well as shared goals with my mate.

❦ Based on past experiences in my childhood, and recent adulthood, I expect life to be happy and my relationships to be fulfilling.

Individually, take time to journal with each statement above. Come together with your mate and take turns listening to your partner. Don't make judgments, sit quietly with your heart open and imagine that you can see the little girl or little boy learning to share from their heart. Be gentle, and realize that you are there as a support for your relationship and for each other.

Play soft music and light a candle, say a prayer, invoke your angels, or whatever feels good and safe to you. You are creating a safe place for deep intimacy. Acknowledge yourself and each other for giving to your relationship and to your future happiness together.

Keep a daily dairy for a month and get in touch with what is working in your life, relationship, and career. Continue to notice what makes you happy: the people, the environment, and activities.

As you become more aware of what brings you happiness you are empowered to make choices to include more in your life. You cannot share what you don't already possess. Part of committing to your relationship is deepening your awareness of what makes you happy. This will begin to expand in your life, relationship, and career.

Being happy inside brings you success, love, and insures your success in "making love."

EFT for Releasing Fear and Letting Go

This EFT exercise is for releasing fear of letting go. Many of you may not know what it feels like to feel safe. If not, it is time to create a safe place in your mind and train your nerves to feel safe to let go. Hold a scene in your mind when you felt afraid. Chart your feelings 0-10. Work to release your fear of letting go. Work daily for a week on feeling safe and learn what feeling safe, feels like for you.

❧ **Begin by tapping on the top of the center of your head. Repeat as you tap,**"Even though I may have a belief that life is not safe, still I choose to deeply and completely love and accept myself and give myself permission to relax and feel safe."

❧ **Tap on the area between your eyebrows, at the inside edge of each eyebrow, above the bridge of your nose. Repeat as you tap,**"Even though I have never experienced feeling safe and I may have made a decision as a little(girl or boy) that the world is not a safe place, still I choose to deeply and completely love and accept myself and give myself permission to learn to relax and feel safe."

☾ Tap on the outside corner of each eye. Repeat as you tap, "This old fear of being hurt, but longing to feel safe and loved, just a survival skill, I started in my childhood causing me to feel anxious and keeping me on alert, still I choose to deeply and completely love and accept myself and give myself permission to relax and let go."

☾ Tap on the outside corner of each nostril. Repeat as you tap, "These are decisions I made as a little (girl or boy) based on the writing on my walls and my past experiences as a child. Just old stories written to create my life journey, and create my life lessons, still I choose to deeply and completely love and accept myself."

☾ Tap on the center of the upper lip just below your nose. Repeat as you tap, "These old fears of letting go of being on alert and feeling anxious. My old habits I created as a little (girl or boy) who longed to feel safe and protected, are just old survival skills, not who I am, I am not my survival skills from my parents or my environment. I can take my power back from my addiction to anxiety and feeling on alert and choose to create a new feeling of being safe, and allow myself to relax and let go, still I choose to deeply and completely love and accept myself."

☾ Tap on the center of the chin just below the lower lip. Repeat as you tap, "Even though I may have told myself that I would die if I relaxed and let go, still I choose to deeply and completely love and accept myself."

𝒞 Tap on the top of the chest at the inside of each clavicle or chest bone, just below your chin where your neck meets your chest. Repeat as you tap, "Even though I long to feel safe and relaxed and dream of creating a loving relationship, I am terrified of being hurt, if I let go and relax. This old pattern of wanting to feel safe, but being terrified to relax, is a pattern that repeats and has control over me, still I deeply and completely love and accept myself."

𝒞 Tap just below your underarm in the armpit area in line with the nipple. Repeat as you tap, "Even though I have beaten myself up with this old belief and pattern, still I deeply and completely love and accept myself and choose to release my fear of letting go. I give myself permission to feel safe to create new patterns and habits of relaxing and feeling safe to let go."

Complete this EFT tapping session, and check inside yourself. Test with the same scale of 0-10. Hold a scene in your mind of past fears and anxiety. How much fear do you have of feeling safe to relax and let go? Check your body to see if you feel a lightening of your normal tightness? Keep working either alone or with your mate to bring the score to zero.

Love's Secret number eight
Keep Passion Alive

Rest in reason -Move in Passion
-Kahlil Gibran

Love and Passion Lost

At fifty, Sam found himself with two divorces and in financial ruin. He had given everything to make his marriages work. He had spent long hours at work to be the perfect husband and breadwinner, and long hours were spent on the weekend to have the most beautiful home in the area.

He never slowed down long enough to build a support system, or to do anything that was just for him. At fifty, he figured that at least half his life had gone by, and he was beginning to feel that his chance for happiness had slipped away. He had lost hope to feel passionate about life again.

Passion and Pain

Love's Secret Number 8 is to keep your fires of passion alive and burning bright. Passion pulls you into relationship, and pain pushes you out of relationship. This is the age-old dance of intimacy and love. It is passed down from our parents and their parents. Couples want to be more intimate with the one they love, but most don't know how to feel safe enough to be loved and supported.

Love's "push-pull dance" is fueled by a desire for love and intimacy, and perpetuated by a fear of the loss of control. Pushing occurs as a survival defense mechanism and has nothing to do with the amount of love felt for your mate. Pulling is urged by the soul in an attempt to feel unified and connected.

The female generally feels much more comfortable with submission to unity, and the male is constantly pulling away to recapture his "male identity." Reacting to his survival instinct, the male feels a need to maintain distance as he pulls away. He feels that if he submits to the union of love, he will lose control, his masculinity, and his freedom.

Even worse, he feels if he submits to the union he will melt and lose his identity. Once he can allow himself to keep his heart open, and experience love's deep unity, he will experience more of himself. It is the ego-mind that is convinced that vulnerability and union mean death.

Auto-Pilot

Sam met Sally in a meditation group and fell head-over-heals in love. Eager to apply the skills I had suggested in our coaching sessions, he practiced deep breathing to calm his mind and be still. Surprised to find someone and petrified that he would make the same mistakes again, he began to look for patterns that had cost him two marriages, and created financial problems.

In Sam's past relationships he made decisions on auto-pilot, reacting from his childhood habits. This had landed him in divorce court twice with deep emotional pain. He never took time to realize what was happening until it was too late.

One of Sam's close friends, who had worked with me, referred him. When he entered my office he was nervous. He said that he really didn't know why he was there or if he believed that I could help him. But he knew he had to make a commitment to his future.

Spiritual Relationship

The enlightened dance of intimacy is learning how to be vulnerable, with an open heart, and experience union without losing yourself. The old model was total loss of identification. The new model is interdependence and allows for deep intimacy, while connecting to deeper parts of your soul.

Each partner in a spiritual relationship learns to find the receptive feminine energy within, clear toxic emotions, and remain open and vulnerable. Once you are successful, you will reach new depths of intimacy and simultaneously find new depths of your soul.

Searching for a Spiritual Connection

Sam grew up attending church every Sunday, but eventually rebelled against any form of organized religion. He knew too many friends who attended church and didn't walk the talk. He saw a lot of them cheating on their wives during the week and going to church on the weekend. Many of them felt that as long as they confessed their sins, they were free to go and do it again.

This philosophy didn't work for Sam. He never cheated on his wife. They just seemed to drift apart and lose their love and respect for each other.

Connecting to Spirit

Even though Sam never felt a connection to the "church," he felt connected to a divine spirit when he was in nature. Nature had been his sanctuary in his toxic childhood. When he went into nature, he felt connected to a higher power and felt safe. In our sessions, I encouraged Sam to go into nature and re-establish his connection.

He made time to practice being "still" and listen within. Shortly after learning to be quiet, he began to feel "inspired." He began to follow his hunches, or his "inner voice." This habit was strong with Sam as a child, and had even saved his life a couple of times.

The first time, he had a dream and saw himself involved in an accident. He woke with a strong sense of fear one morning and decided to stay home that day. If he had gone to work he would have been on the two lane highway where a horrible accident took the lives of two friends. It shook him to his core. The second time it happened and he followed his "inner direction" he felt it was too weird and shut down.

Learning to Trust Again

In our coaching sessions we released fears and blocks to love and also to Sam's ability to trust himself and inner guidance. Sam was one of the special people who were born with natural powers to see and hear. As a child, he was so open that he could see and hear thoughts and pictures in the minds of the people around him. This was pretty scary for a young child, so he shut it and his feelings down.

He had made a decision that it wasn't safe to feel or see anything. Living his life shut down had become too painful to continue, he had to learn a new way to exist, or die. He was chronically depressed and anxious most of the time, and didn't know how to change it.

Pain is a Wake-up Call for Change

Sam felt years of physical pain lifted from his shoulders as we removed chronic holding patterns of stress and constriction in his muscles. With each session he felt stronger and began to trust himself to feel and see again.

He learned how to trust himself and use his special "gifts" to help him and others.

Sally Arrives

Sam was feeling good again and was in touch with a new passion for life. He was using his special gifts as a medical intuitive and found the ability to see inside the people who came to him. Through meditation, yoga, and EFT he had tools to keep himself centered and opened up to his special gifts. He no longer needed to distance himself and beat himself up by attracting women who were not emotionally available.

He met Sally just at the right time. She was in marketing and graphic arts, and enjoyed helping the people she met in the holistic community. Sam was in need of someone who could help him promote himself and build his practice. Their meeting was destined, and included more than just help with his career. When their eyes met, they experienced a deep sense of connection, and felt they had found their life partner.

A Divine Partnership

Sally was searching for someone like Sam, who was ready for a divine partnership. She had been practicing meditation to build inner peace and was ready for a conscious relationship. Armed with new skills of communication and tools to keep them on track, they planned their life together and set a wedding date.

Patty and Dave's Story

At the beginning of their relationship Patty and Dave felt deep love and passion, yet now they felt miles apart and lonely. Even though they had felt the distance, they were still totally committed to their relationship.

The grass looked greener on the other side, but both were experienced enough to realize that this was the ego's need to run away, rather than negotiate and find a solution. It had been five years and more and more distance had crept between them. Many couples get lost at this point in a marriage and just decide to call it quits. Patty and Dave knew they had a strong foundation for a good marriage, but they didn't have tools to create it.

Passion was Alive

At the beginning of the relationship, they couldn't wait to get home. They had fantasized about the love they would make that evening. Their love and intimacy was something they both enjoyed and valued. Then, old habits of distancing crept in, along with a pregnancy and birth of their first child. Eventually the distance was accepted as a part of the relationship. Their intimacy had been lost, not because they had consciously chosen it, but because they had neglected to make their love a priority.

Distance Kills Passion

Patty and Dave's marriage didn't look bad from the outside. They each had good jobs and they shared chores at home and with the children. Passion had disappeared among the diapers and chores.

They longed for more intimacy and to feel connected like they did in the beginning. But neither of them had taken the initiative to create it. This seemed to stem from a belief that eventually it would come back together. After all, they did love each other.

Patty's fear was that the distance might become permanent and they might lose the relationship altogether. While surfing the Internet, Patty found information on a retreat for couples. The retreat sounded intriguing and seemed like it might be the answer to her prayers. She and Dave had not had a week away from the kids in three years, and she was excited to think of time alone.

Finding Support

Patty was excited, but how would she convince Dave to spend the money right now? Their finances were tight. She devised a plan to cut down on restaurant meals for a few months and save money. Dave was receptive to the idea, and welcomed the time alone with Patty without distraction. Excited to spend time together, they scheduled the retreat, and put a deposit down. Anxious to move forward, they prepaid and received preparation materials. The couple had some preliminary work to do before the retreat.

A Vision

They received their packet of homework. Their first process was to individually create a vision of how they wanted their relationship. This was thought provoking for them. Neither had considered what they wanted in a relationship. It was just supposed to evolve and they were supposed to be together for the rest of their lives. Both sets of parents were divorced, but they had decided that they would never give into divorce. Yet, as they took stock of their relationship, they saw that possibility if they didn't make some needed changes.

Following Roles from Their Past

Patty was a beautiful, take-charge person. She loved organization. Dave was more than willing to allow Patty to keep their life organized and give her that power. Dave, kept busy with two jobs, and was usually gone, from sun up to sun down. He was never aware of how much money was in the bank or generally where the money was being budgeted and spent. He just made sure there was plenty in their account.

Dave enjoyed making love to Patty, but was so exhausted from his life and work that he rarely felt the urge anymore. Patty was beginning to take this personally, wondering if he was having an affair. But she knew that he didn't really have time for an affair. The logical conclusion drawn from her subconscious mind was that he wasn't attracted to her anymore.

Heart Expressions

Their homework included "heart expression" sessions in preparation for the retreat. Patty was surprised to learn that Dave was still attracted to her and that he did still desire her. Relieved and dismissing her inner fears, Patty had new hope and began to feel comfortable again to communicate her feelings. During their "heart expression" session, Dave shared that he missed their lovemaking. He explained to Patty that he was just too exhausted, but felt guilty because he wasn't performing his duty.

They had not made intimacy a priority. They made a commitment to change their priorities, as they realized their future happiness depended on it. Sadness filled their hearts, because they didn't like the distance they felt between them. Getting caught up in day-to-day life, they had allowed all their time, energy, and money, to be used for other things.

Making Love and Intimacy a Priority

They spent time examining their budgeting and where their money was spent. Patty realized in planning their budget, her focus had not made love and intimacy a priority.

She shifted her focus and made intimacy and their relationship their first priority. She found a book recommended in her outside reading list from the retreat, called "Your Money or Your Life." This book had her look at money as life energy, and then helped her prioritize how she spent that energy.

A Fresh Awareness

Having shifted priorities, Patty examined her life and relationship with a fresh awareness. Her new focus for building their budget was to shift from a materialistic point to creating a lasting, loving environment in her home and marriage. If she wanted quality time with her husband, she now realized it was equally her responsibility to create it.

Patty and Dave had done their individual homework for the retreat well ahead of time, and kept their journals daily. As a couple, they were learning to take responsibility for their lives and create what they wanted.

Continuing on auto-pilot and blindly arriving in divorce court was not the destination they wanted. Their parents had expected their own marriages to mature and evolve in a good direction, but they ended in disaster.

Both of their parents felt victimized and helpless to change their life and it ended in divorce. Their relationships didn't meet their expectations, but they never realized why. It had proved hopeless for them with their emotional hurt and pain, to forgive the past and move on. Each set of parents was still stewing in feelings of hurt, resentment, and anger. They were unwilling to do the healing needed to release them and claim a happier life.

Renewed Passion

Patty and Dave were happy and feeling relief that they had found a new path to create a happy, fulfilling, and lasting relationship. In the beginning they had both felt uncomfortable confronting their habits and changing their life. The money invested in the retreat, and their pain of shutting down, motivated them to change their destructive patterns.

Moving through the fear of self-confrontation and facing the fear of change was now paying off. By making time for intimacy and enjoying quality time together, they noticed a new joy in their daily life.

New passion and excitement was stirring within them, and they couldn't wait to learn even more techniques to enhance their lives and their relationship.

Excitement Stirs

Patty and Dave were so excited to have a week alone, they felt like newlyweds again. The beauty of Sedona was breath-taking. They met nine other couples very similar to their backgrounds. Most had been married for a few years and had slipped into some negative habits. The group of couples, whether newly weds or seasoned honeymooners, was committed to take their relationships to a new level of intimacy.

Each had been journaling and completing homework. They had already learned a great deal about themselves, as well as their mate. Each couple had a deep level of love and commitment, and they each had their own individual challenges within their relationships.

New Tools for Relating

The beauty and peace of the Sedona environment put each of the couples at ease, and they felt safe to share from a deep level. The group leader knew just how to weave laughter, shared stories of heartbreak, and individual goals and dreams, to assist them in finding new levels of their relationship.

Each couple shared a vision for their relationship, and they began to notice common threads interwoven in each vision. It was comforting to find that many couples experienced the same challenges in keeping their love and commitment alive and growing.

Patty and Dave were feeling deeper levels of love than they had experienced in years. Shutting down their hearts was a survival instinct that each learned as a child, and was still a strong reaction when either of them felt they were not being heard or understood. In addition to shutting down, they found an irresistible urge to push the other person away.

Distancing habits had created barriers for their love and the relationship they envisioned. Through role-playing and other techniques, they were able to look at these habits with new eyes and from a new perspective. They learned to make new decisions to support love, rather than blindly reacting from old habits.

Love Restored

Renewed love, open hearts and minds, and a new understanding of their mate, gave them tools to keep their relationship on course. Every one of the couples agreed that the week together had been the best time and money they had invested in their marriage.

They all agreed their lives might be different if they had received the training and knowledge before their marriage began. The bad habits would never have been started and they would have experienced many more "love" moments.

Love's Secret by Patty and Dave

❧ Commit to your own happiness and relationship, or it might be doomed to repeat patterns and end in divorce.

❧ Create a different story with awareness and confront your past.

🌜 You can lose sight of what is most important and create a disaster in your own life and relationship.

🌜 Just because you want a happy life and relationship doesn't mean you are equipped to create it.

🌜 Love habits support love and heart connections. Care enough to develop the discipline to make love habits a part of your daily life.

🌜 Make your love and relationship a priority rather than focusing on material possessions.

Contemplating the Story

🌜 Write in your journal about what you feel from Patty and Dave's story.

🌜 What touched your heart?

🌜 Do you have habits that stand in your way of creating more intimacy?

🌜 Are you making your relationship a priority?

Love's Secret to Ignite Passion

🌜 You control the reins of passion by the thoughts held in your mind.

🌜 You are the only one who can find what makes you feel passionately alive.

🌜 Constant busy-ness, without taking time to evaluate

what you want, keeps you entangled in a web that drains your inner passion.

❧ When your thoughts and actions are focused on acceptance and acknowledgement, it is easy to stay passionately in love.

❧ Awareness and discipline help you change the habits drowning out passion and pushing love and intimacy out of your life.

❧ When there is a lack of passion in your relationship one or both partners have closed down and are withholding love.

❧ Once both of you are fully engaged and giving to each other, the passion magically returns.

Igniting Your Inner Passion

A belief that passion is created outside you is a misdirected idea. Passion and its blissful chemicals come from within, and are stimulated by your thoughts. Passion comes from being actively engaged in life and being connected to Divine Source, and then channeling that energy into something you love. Once connected to source, your relationship can be a channel for creative flow.

In order to use your relationship as a channel for creative life force, you must keep excitement alive and keep your channels of communication open. To build

and maintain passion with your partner, you must nurture your own inner passion. Awareness will help you
develop habits that build inner passion and keep the
embers of your inner fire glowing.

Love's Secret number nine
Focus on Love

Your living is determined not so much by what life brings to you as by the attitude you bring to life; not so much by what happens to you as by the way your mind looks at what happens.

-KAHLIL GIBRAN

Patience, Persistence, and Being Present

Lynn had spent most of her life running from case to case and never took time to realize she wasn't present.

As a prominent lawyer, she had an intimidating presence that she always presented in the courtroom. But the ability to be present? She didn't have a clue what I was referring to!

Being Present

Love's Secret Number 9 is to be patient with yourself and your mate. As you persistently learn to be present and hold your focus on love, you develop the ability to choose your actions. This means you must give up auto-pilot mode. You then notice everywhere you look, friends and family playing out roles as victims to their own mind. They have addictions to out dated beliefs and toxic emotions. Having owned your past and bringing your actions and reactions current with your present choices, you find it hard to allow their misery in your life.

Many feel victimized by society and their lives and feel hopeless for improvement in their lives. The largest segments of society remain caught in the rat race, and never stop to realize the source of their unhappiness, or how to change their situation.

In this chapter you will find tools to assist you to be present and enjoy the moment. You will learn to anchor yourself into your body and become comfortable with being "in the moment". Pull yourself back from fearing the future or wasting time on past regrets. Develop the discipline to stay present.

"Experience inner peace by leaving the past behind, allowing the future to joyfully unfold, and gift yourself the 'present' of the moment."

-ANNIE LAWRENCE

Stressful Work Environment

Lynn's work environment was filled with stress and she had adapted by building a thick "skin." She worked daily with women who were seeking a large settlement from their divorce, and were totally stressed. She had one of the largest law firms in the area and was known for "closing the case with a good settlement and fast." She wasn't intimidated by the highest powered male attorney. Many of them had at one time or another been her lover, and she enjoyed "getting" their male "goat."

Despite her success and hot sex life, she had a deep question that plagued her. Was she happy? If not, what was it that was lacking? She had exceeded her goals and dreams and didn't understand her depression. Her mind was constantly churning over her unhappiness and inner turmoil. Lynn had been diagnosed as chronically depressed and her doctor prescribed Zoloft. She found it easier to pop a pill than slow down and find out why she was unhappy.

We met over the phone through a referral from a mutual friend. Lynn liked the fact that we could work by phone and that I wasn't a part of her local social crowd. She needed help but didn't want anyone to know. Being vulnerable is not something that Lynn allowed herself to display within her social group.

Shut Down

Sometimes you may have shut down for so long that you lose touch with your emotions. As they begin to surface you don't recognize what is happening. You know that there is a sense of something wrong, perhaps a deep sense of sadness. You learn to push it down with work, sex, alcohol, anti-depressant pills or whatever will give the quickest relief. Fifty percent of the women who visit our retreat center (98% are women) are on some form of anti-depressant drugs. Recently I saw a report that said $60 billion were spent on anti-depressant drugs in the ninety's.

Drugs Numb Emotions

Lynn had been on anti-depressants and a sleep inducing drug for four years. She kept herself so busy she told herself she didn't have time to stop and 'catch up' with her emotions. Constant pressure to win a case and get it settled had finally pushed her over the edge. She felt herself on the verge of mental, emotional, and physical exhaustion. A break-down is not something that would enhance her career.

A Break

Lynn decided to take a break. In our first phone consultation she said she was terrified inside and had no idea why.

In sharing her childhood, she said it was average, with no red flags of abuse that she could remember. Her mom had always encouraged her to pursue her career and had never pushed for a traditional family life with grandkids. All Lynn knew was that her eyes felt as though someone turned on the faucet and forgot to turn it off. She wondered if she should call her doctor and get her antidepressants changed or increased. Even though she hated crying, she felt lighter with a deep sense of relief.

Break-downs: an 'Inner Cry' for Change

I shared my own view of the process that Lynn was experiencing. Her life was not happy; she had been pushing emotions down for years with various numbing agents. Crying for attention, her body wanted and needed relief from the emotional burdens it had carried for years. It was time to listen to her inner voice and allow herself a needed 'time out.' Otherwise she could have more serious mental, emotional or physical symptoms appear.

She agreed, and asked for help in navigating the emotional dam that had been released. It was hard for Lynn to be quiet and listen inside; she didn't like what she found.

As we worked, we found buried anger toward her mom and dad. They had never been emotionally available. Lynn shut down to avoid feeling the hurt and rejection and learned to focus her attention outward.

We released fear of being present and moved a lot of buried hurt, shame, and guilt. Lynn had a private yoga teacher working with her and was receiving massages daily throughout her 'time out.' Her body was responding to her new attention and she was beginning to feel lighter.

Lynn agreed to fly in for a week-long retreat with us so that we could concentrate our efforts and move the emotions more quickly. When she arrived she looked pale and anxious. Vulnerability was still not welcomed. She liked the comfort of her tough skin and the familiar comfort of her cloak of denial.

Being Patient

Habits of shutting down and protecting with layers of denial are a familiar pattern. When love and nurturing are not offered as a child the child learns to adapt. Patterns of shutting down and denying emotions are not healthy, and will end in either physical or emotional disease if not changed.

One of the main stress inducers is change. You may have 'thick skin' and feel that you can pop a pill and continue your life without facing your unhealthy habits. Confronting your carefully-protected denial and habits may feel like a pending death sentence. Denial and habits of shutting down will have to die, in order for you to grow and change and learn to be happy. Patience is required as you learn to shed your thick skin.

Lynn felt uncomfortable feeling her emotions coming off auto-pilot and out of shut down and denial. But she was making progress daily. Daily yoga and meditation had become a welcomed tool for staying centered. She had added breath breaks throughout her day and was learning to master her breath, which had been shallow and constricted for years.

Each day she gained strength and we removed more layers of old emotional pain and denial of pain. She looked ten years younger and had gained lightness to her appearance. Feeling more confident and centered, she began to feel comfortable to be present, and now had an understanding of what 'being present' means.

Persistence

As you change inside, your outer world will change. This will require releasing baggage from your life, including friends, and perhaps limiting the time you spend around your family. Everyone wakes up at different times. Your friends and family may wake up and decide to be happy or they may remain stuck. You must evaluate everything in your life, including relationships, work, and your environment. You are a spiritual being in a physical body and environment. Life is your playground to evolve and grow.

Your life lesson is to wake up and create inner peace and happiness, rather than stay stuck in turmoil and your self-created hell.

-ANNIE LAWRENCE

Focus on Being Happy

❦ Stay happy 'inside' by being present and choosing your thoughts. Keep an 'inner thoughts' journal. This allows you to monitor your progress and stay on track.

❦ Monitor your thoughts and actions on a moment-to-moment basis. Focused thoughts are an anchor to create the life of your dreams. Being aware of your thoughts allows you to focus your thoughts on what you want. Keep your journal for a month and notice how your life changes.

❦ Create a dream board. Make pictures of what you want to create, in three months, six months, and a year.

❦ Life requires work whether you decide to be happy, or remain stuck in self-defeating turmoil and unhappiness. Make the effort to change and grow.

❦ Moment to moment be aware of emotions and interactions. Make new choices for thoughts and actions. Grow into a more rewarding life.

❦ There is discomfort in the beginning and you must face your fear in choosing to grow.

❦ Growth takes you into areas of uncertainty, and can create anxiety and nervous tension.

Evaluating and Acknowledging Success

Set aside time to be quiet and undisturbed. Turn off the cell phone, the landline, and all outside disturbances.

Light a candle and set your intention. Ask for inner guidance to help you evaluate your progress.

Acknowledge your success in acting and reacting to life differently. Take inventory of where you are with your inner relationship, with your thoughts and inner voice, and with your outer relationship.

Take a moment to acknowledge your success by jotting down the strengths you notice. Good indications of change and growth are: inner peace, calm mind, and you find it easier to enter your peaceful space inside. You are happy most of the time.

Hold a vision in your mind of love habits getting stronger. Feel inner trust and confidence within you grow stronger. Feel gratitude for the new you growing inside.

Look at the challenges you continue to confront. For example, beating yourself up with your inner critic, or reacting and then getting angry because you fall into old habits.

New challenges will emerge as you gain strength to face them. Consider any new challenges that arise as growth opportunities.

Take time for this inner evaluation individually, and then come together as a couple and share your reflections. Give positive feedback about what you see that has changed over the past weeks and months, in each other and your relationship.

Share the success you see within your relationship first. Then give constructive feedback by asking from the heart for what you want more of in your interactions and relating.

Remember to ask with statements like, "I really enjoy _____ and would like to have this in our relationship. I would love to schedule this and make time for it."

Make sure that when you ask for something and receive it, you acknowledge it. Give something to your partner that you know they enjoy receiving in return. Don't set up a check and measure system. Develop the habit of feeling joy from giving.

Continuous Emotional Healing

A spiritual relationship brings joy and takes a lot of commitment and discipline of the mind and emotions. In this partnership there is continuous surfacing of old hurts to be embraced and healed. This is like peeling an onion: you continue to deal with deeper and deeper hurts as you feel safer and more comfortable.

Deep commitment to your own healing and to the partnership become a strong foundation for your healing journey. By now you are feeling more comfortable in your inner world and have developed tools to avoid getting lost in the protective maze of old patterns. The rewards are clarity, and happiness, and moving out of self-destructive patterns of the past. You are moving away from the addiction to toxic emotions and their chemicals, and reaping rewards of inner and outer joy and renewed passion.

Stay on Track by Staying Current

"By spending time in reviewing your present situation you will find clues as to what is lurking under the surface and ready to be embraced and healed.

"When you take responsibility for your situation, support will surround you to help in your healing. You will find yourself being led to teachers, friendships, groups, and support systems to guide your steps. Trust your inner guidance, commit to being present, and take the steps necessary to embrace the happy life you deserve.

Quiet Contemplation

Set aside a time to be quiet and undisturbed. Light a candle and set your intention. Ask for inner guidance to become aware of current emotions that are being repeated in your life. You may notice these patterns repeating in your home life, work environment, and relationships. Stay current with your 'inner healing' and watch your happiness, health, and relationship grow more rewarding than you have ever experienced or imagined.

Inner Life Review

Imagine for a moment that you can become light and begin to float above your life. Invite your guide or angel to be there with you. Perhaps a relative that has passed over and exists only in the light dimensions might guide your journey. Some feel more comfortable with their favorite pet. As you look down at your life, imagine that you can see an overview.

Start your journey in your youth and continue to your current life events.

Look for patterns you repeat in your life. Like a personality who has caused you grief over and over. This personality most resembles which parent or person who was responsible for you?

What lessons have you learned from dealing with this personality? Find your gift.

Do you need to release this person and personality from your life by forgiving them?

What emotions are you holding about this person?

Inner Healing Journey

☾ Before you leave your quiet space, do some journaling regarding what you have learned.

☾ Spend time reviewing you past and take inventory of what needs completion.

☾ Before you blow out your candle complete the following exercise.

☾ If this person has abused you physically, emotionally, or sexually, ask your angels to assist you with this healing. You are doing this for yourself, not for the person you are forgiving. It does not make what they did okay. A wise teacher told his student, holding on to anger is like drinking poison and hoping the other person will die. These people have created their own hell and karma with their actions, and they will reap their own rewards. You are clearing your path so that you can end patterns in your life and stop inner turmoil.

☾ See the person who needs to be released in front of you, and their inner-child beside them. Recognize the hurt they felt as a child, look into their eyes or the eyes of the child, and repeat these words; I love you, I love me, I forgive you and I forgive me, I release you and I release me, now and throughout all time lines and throughout eternity. Feel all the past hurt and pain surrounding this person and then see them and the pain being lifted into the light with the angels. As you feel the old hurt and pain lift from your body, allow your angels to bring in love and light to fill the space that was occupied by the pain, hurt, anger, and guilt.

Find Your Gift

Sit and feel the new light and love within. Allow yourself to find the gift that you gained from this lesson.

There is always a gift, no matter how painful and traumatic the lesson. It may have given you empathy to work with others who have deep pain and trauma, or it may have given you strength and an undefeatable courage to rise against the most horrible odds. In the beginning, it is hard to find the gift and even harder to look at this lesson as a gift. Don't push it; just allow your awareness to bubble up from inside. Continue to be in the moment and wait for the awareness to enter your consciousness.

Peaceful Loving Environment

Make journaling a part of your daily life. It helps you take ownership of your thoughts and actions. It is a tool to develop discipline to create new reactions to life and continue to experience more and more happiness. You will notice old patterns of pushing love away are safely put in the past. Gentleness, compassion, understanding, and sharing from your heart are a welcome part of your daily life.

Pain is No Longer a Requirement for Growth

In the past it may have taken a crisis in your life, making your life so painful that you could no longer bear it, for you to wake up and make a decision to change. Be happy that pain is no longer a requirement for your growth.

Patience is Passion tamed.

-KAHLIL GIBRAN

Tim was working with our men's group, which was committed to taming their addiction to sex and passionate relationships. Most of these men had been propelled by an unknown force that seemed stronger than they were. This strong force attracted women who were very beautiful, passionate, and uninhibited sexually. Neither the women nor the men seemed to be able to make the relationships last longer than a year. At the one-year anniversary, both partners seemed to get bored and ready for a new, more passionate partner.

Tim and the men in the group had made a commitment to develop the skill to create a long-term relationship. Their group leader asked them to make a list of what they were looking for in a life partner. Then they were to examine their own personalities to see if they could find these qualities within themselves. The men were to do deep soul-searching and discover which patterns they each brought to their relationships.

Addicted to Passion

Addicted to passion, each man discovered that none had ever really been in love. They had mistaken their addiction to love's euphoric chemical high, for 'being' in love.

Tim looked for the reasons he hid behind sex and passion. He wanted to find the root of his addiction to sex. As he searched for the root of his addiction, he learned that the flood of endorphins associated with love and sex were just as addictive as any drug. When the chemical rush slowed and old layers of toxic emotions emerged

Tim found reasons to move on. He was amazed to find his drug of choice was self-created through sex.

Fear of Intimacy

Tim longed to be in love and find someone with whom he felt comfortable holding and being held. He had always looked at his childhood as being fairly happy, and didn't seem to have any memories of being abused in any way.

Yet he felt uncomfortable with touching, being alone, and spending quality time with his mate. He always kept a busy schedule. When he spent time with his mate of the moment he had a plan. This plan never included much intimacy, but it sure included a lot of quick and passionate sex.

The sex that he enjoyed was spontaneous, quick, and never included much foreplay or any cuddling afterwards. It was always get dressed quickly for dinner out, or a movie, or whatever the night on the town included.

Life in the fast lane had always been exciting for Tim. His career and his many encounters had never left much room for contemplation, until one day when he woke up and realized that something was very wrong. He felt a very large hole in his life. He had never made time for friends and he had never bothered to keep in touch with any of his past encounters. He realized that he didn't know how to be intimate or have a spiritual connection, and both now seemed to be urgently important.

Attracting Love not Lust

Each man in the group, made a list of what they want-ed in a life partner. Then they looked for the attributes within their own personalities. They were all lacking in the qualities that they found most important. The top quality they wanted and valued most was to be heard and understood.

Reacting to life on auto-pilot, without awareness, each man moved through life quickly between encounters and their careers. They had avoided their pain and inner feel-ings of separation and loneliness. Old patterns of moving toward love and then pushing it away had taken its toll. They all had good careers, but most had more debt and liabilities than money or assets.

Financial and Emotional Disaster

The revolving door of beautiful, sexy women had taken a toll on each man, both financially and emo-tionally. It was a pass-time that easily kept their attention in youth. Now their lives were empty and filled with remorse.

The men entered the group in hopes of welcoming intimacy into their lives for the first time in more than fifty years. In the beginning, it was hard for them to slow down their minds and become present.

Commitment to Heal

Tim could not figure out which was more uncomfortable, his painful life as it existed, or being a part of the group. Being present and choosing to grow was full of confrontation and feelings he would rather have left in the past. This change was necessary if he wanted friendships and to find a life partner. But it brought with it anxiety and fear.

Learning to Listen

Tim had finally learned to be present. This was a quality that his new partner Denise found very attractive. She had been working on herself for many years, and had been longing for a life partner willing to do his personal healing. She had made her own list of the qualities that she was looking for in a mate.

She was pleased that she saw all those qualities in Tim. Our men's group had given Tim both the ability to listen, hear, and understand, and give feedback regarding her life. Denise valued this and it helped to establish a deep bond between them. For the first time in each of their lives, they felt heard, understood, and valued. Each felt a friendship growing, in addition to the passion; this was exciting for them.

Patience and Persistence

Emotional baggage was present for both Denise and

Tim to heal, but they were equally prepared and committed to heal. Tim was learning compassionate communication through our men's group and Denise had studied it years before. When issues came to the surface to be healed, they had techniques to resolve it.

They found themselves doing deep healing within their young relationship. Viewing their union as a divine meeting of two souls drawn together to facilitate healing, they had deep respect for each other.

Humor Adds Joy

They looked at their differences with respect and gratitude. They knew those differences brought their own unique gifts. Each ripple in their blissful sea of happiness brought tremendous growth, and opportunities to laugh and lighten up. One of the joyful qualities that they both cherished was the humor they each brought to the relationship.

Denise and Tim had created a vision of what they wanted in their relationship. Tim found our men's group a good support for him and their relationship, while Denise had a meditation group that she found useful.

Love's Secret by Denise and Tim

By working through the process of creating their unified vision, they held realistic views of what each person wanted to receive.

Compassionate communication prepared them for negotiations and helped to keep them focused as a team, rather than fighting for control.

Their vision created a strong intent to guide them through the emotional storms and upheavals, and kept them focused on love. It became a road map to keep them connected to their love, rather than getting lost in the twisted roads of past hurt.

They had each committed to take time to do personal inventory each day and stay current with their feelings and emotions. This commitment helped them to avoid explosions of emotions that might derail them on their journey.

Denise and Tim had learned to be empathetic listeners and negotiate their individual needs. They developed a grateful heart.

Contemplating the Story

☾ Go to your quiet space and seek your inner guidance. Practice the ritual that you have found most effective to connect with your wisdom.

☾ Have your journal ready, and take time to breathe and relax. Reflect on the questions below and allow your answers to flow from you heart.

☾ Do you have a support group to air your concerns outside your relationship and receive support and guidance?

☾ If not, perhaps this is a good time to begin your search for a space where you can feel supported.

☾ As you seek out your group, notice any resistance.

☾ Perhaps you have always been a loner. Remember you are learning that your old story is just a story and not who you are.

☾ Being a loner is just a habit and you can choose new habits based on your needs and wants of today.

☾ Shift your focus from despair to prayer and ask for help and assistance. You will find answers showing up everywhere; take action on what shows up.

☾ Welcome and acknowledge the little miracles around every corner and lifelines of hope being thrown all around you. Reach out and say "Yes" to the miracles and take hold of the lifelines. You can choose inner peace and create a life of love and happiness.

EFT for Releasing Old Pictures

This is an EFT exercise to release old pictures and beliefs that caused you to attract lust instead of love. Hold a scene in your mind of what you think love should look like. Is it realistic? Is this just another way of sabotaging yourself and your partner by having unrealistic pictures and hidden agendas? Use the EFT phrases below to find any unrealistic pictures or hidden expectations that might sabotage your love and partnership.

 Begin by tapping on the top of the center of your head. Repeat as you tap, "Even though I may have a belief that love needs to be passionate and new to be exciting, still I choose to deeply and completely love and accept myself."

 Tap on the area between your eyebrows, at the inside edge of each eyebrow, above the bridge of your nose. Repeat as you tap, "Even though I might have old movies of how love is suppose to look, and may have made a decision as a young person that love must be hot and lusty to be exciting, still I choose to deeply and completely love and accept myself."

 Tap on the outside corner of each eye. Repeat as you tap, "This old addiction to hot passionate sex that I use to judge my relationships and push intimacy away, while longing for deep intimacy, are just pictures created at an immature stage of past relationships and cause me to push love away, still I choose to deeply and completely love and accept myself.?

 Tap on the outside corner of each nostril. Repeat as you tap, "These decisions I made as a young immature person based on the writing on my walls and my past experiences, are just old stories written to create my life journey, and create my life lessons, still I choose to deeply and completely love and accept myself."

⟲ **Tap on the center of the upper lip just below your nose. Repeat as you tap,** "These old fears of intimacy and being stuck in self-sabotage by my old inner movies of lust and sex. I choose to take my power back from my addiction to lust and passion that keeps me stuck longing for love and deep intimacy. Still I choose to deeply and completely love and accept myself."

⟲ **Tap on the center of the chin just below the lower lip. Repeat as you tap,** "Even though I may have made a vow to myself that I would never allow myself to be stuck in a relationship without passionate sex, still I choose to deeply and completely love and accept myself and examine my inner pictures of what love is and looks like."

⟲ **Tap on the top of the chest at the inside of each clavicle or chest bone just below your chin where your neck meets your chest. Repeat as you tap,** "Even though sex is modeled to me as love and I may not know what love looks like or how to sustain authentic love, still I deeply and completely love and accept myself and give myself permission to create new pictures of what I want love to look like for my partnership."

⟲ **Tap just below your underarm in the armpit area in line with the nipple. Repeat as you tap,** "Even though I may have searched everywhere for the perfect mate and beat myself up with this old belief and pattern, still I deeply and completely love and accept myself and choose to release my old decisions and pictures of love and open my heart to experience authentic love. I give myself permission to feel safe to create new pictures and habits that support love."

Check inside yourself and notice your feelings. Test your feelings with the same scale of 0-10. Hold a scene in your mind of being addicted to the chase for the perfect mate. How much fear do you have of being present to experience deep love and intimacy? Keep working either alone or with your mate to bring the score to zero.

Love's Secret number ten
CELEBRATE LOVE

Love many things, for therein lies the true strength, and whoso-ever loves much performs much, and can accomplish much, and what is done in love is done well.

-VINCENT VAN GOGH

Ecstatic and grateful, Trudy felt she had been given a second chance to experience spiritual love. Trudy met Freeman and they were euphoric with happiness. They were determined to create love habits to support their new love.

Love's Secret Number 10 is to celebrate love each day. Be present and practice "love habits" and choose to celebrate love with each action.

Trudy and Freeman's Journey to Love

Trudy had a birthday last week; she just turned fifty. She feels as young and vibrant as she did at thirty-five. In love with her life, and now she found someone to share that love. Trudy has not always been in love with her life; she was quite miserable for the first forty years. She was married just out of high school and immediately got pregnant. This meant that Trudy never had a chance to even consider college or a career.

Trudy was a typical stay-at-home mom and focused most of her attention on her family. At age thirty, she woke up and found herself miserable. She felt her husband and children took her, and all the love and care she provided for them, for granted. Trudy loved her family very much but felt that something very big was missing from her life. She lacked a sense self-worth and needed to find more meaning for her life.

Searching for Deeper Meaning

Growing up in a strict and devout Catholic home, Trudy had her fair share of guilt. Through her growth and reevaluation of her life she no longer abides by the strict rules imposed by her childhood religion. Recently she had decided to expand her knowledge and explore other ways of connecting to her spiritual side. First she took a meditation class at a local non-denominational church.

She found the meditation class very self-confronting, and had a very hard time getting beyond mind chatter. She picked up a flyer that she found very intriguing and couldn't get it out of her mind. The flyer was advertising a part-time career as a massage therapist. Trudy had never considered massage as a career, nor had she ever received a massage. Yet, it sounded like something that might give her some extra cash and she loved the thought of helping others feel better.

Expanding with New Awareness

Trudy never imagined she could learn so much about the body and about herself in two short weeks. She took Tai Chi classes each day, and learned about anatomy. All the classes released emotions and memories from her childhood. She had entered the class hoping to help others, but she found her own life totally transformed. The massage class ended and her clinic internship began. With each massage, Trudy felt her self-confidence and self-esteem grow.

Tai Chi remained a part of her daily life along with breath work and meditation. Her mind had slowed down and she had a new inner peace and connection to spirit. Trudy found herself becoming happier than she had been in years. But she felt further and further distanced from her husband.

Searching for Inner Peace

Trudy missed the support system in the school and found herself wanting to take more classes. She had never experienced such a loving supportive atmosphere that the massage school and clinic offered. She felt so open and free to be herself there, but felt very controlled and restricted in her home.

Her husband began to complain about meals not being prepared when he arrived home, and demanded that she discontinue her classes. He didn't feel they needed extra money from the massages and he gave Trudy an ultimatum. Either she stay home "where she belonged" or he was going to move out. Trudy found the decision easy to make and asked him to leave. For some time she suspected that he had someone else on the side. Now she felt the confidence to break the tie that held her in an unhealthy relationship.

Trudy had a rough few years being a single mom and learning to balance child-rearing with her new career. Once she finished her training and opened her own studio, she found herself more available emotionally for her children. Her home felt much more peaceful and loving, and her children responded by being more supportive. They now worked together as a team to create a happy supportive place to live.

Renewed Passion for Life

Trudy was very happy and in love with life. She had a bright glow of energy around her. She was so busy with her life, business, and children that she hadn't really thought about being alone when she met Freeman. Freeman was kind and thoughtful and just the right person for Trudy. He was a member of Trudy's meditation class, which she had included in her life since she had graduated from massage school.

A New Relationship

With their children grown and ready to enter college, both were ready to think about themselves and a relationship. Each had remnants of past relationships to release, so they could begin fresh, with a clean slate. At the very beginning of their relationship, they attended a weekend retreat, and found new tools to create a good, solid foundation for their relationship.

They loved each other more deeply than they had experienced before and wanted to assure success this time. Their goal was a relationship that could grow with them and support their growth. Both were mature enough to recognize their differences and the beauty the differences offered. There was only one problem; both were attached to their respective house and life style and found it hard to compromise.

Negotiating Needs

Freeman had been very successful and had a beautiful oceanfront home. It offered plenty of room for Trudy and her one son who was now a senior in high school. Trudy had lived in her house for thirty-five years and had raised her children there. This home was inland in the mountains, and was close to her son's school and her massage studio. Freeman didn't understand why she didn't want to stop doing massage and retire and live near the ocean.

It had taken Trudy many years to develop her clientele and she enjoyed her work very much. It was a large and enjoyable part of her life, and she valued the interactions with her clients. Her clients had become her extended family. Giving massage had become a part of Trudy's spiritual practice, and she was not ready to completely give it up. This pushed a very deep button in Trudy, and brought memories of her first husband and his control tactics. Trudy loved Freeman very much and she wanted a life partner, but wondered if they could compromise and work it out.

Merging Lives

Deeply in love and sharing common life goals, Trudy and Freeman had to reach a compromise. Freeman had asked Trudy to marry him in July after graduation and she had accepted. Their differences didn't appear until after they began planning their life together. It was as if a bomb had dropped in their peaceful love-filled lives. Not wanting to feel their hurt and pain, they reacted and shut down. Each felt all the pain that had not been dealt with and completed from past hurts and relationships.

Trudy remembered the weekend retreat they had attended at the beginning of the relationship. She called her coach and booked a retreat for the next weekend. She was so hurt and in so much pain; she realized that she needed a lifeline from somewhere soon. The retreat and their coach were a perfect solution; they already had a connection to the coach and could work through the pain and patterns that had them stuck.

Seeking Support

Both Trudy and Freeman were still committed to each other and trusted that they would find a solution during the retreat. The coach had them go back to their relationship vision and sit and meditate together. Once they were both more centered and had reestablished their heart connection they began to look for solutions and compromise. They were to hold each other that evening and set the problems aside. Each of them was to ask for solutions to be revealed in their dreams, then meditate first thing in the morning and write for an hour.

In their morning coaching session, they had found a new willingness to compromise. Freeman had realized how much Trudy loved her work and was encouraging her to find ways to include it in their new life. Trudy knew that she didn't have to work unless she wanted and that if she sold her house, she would be able to build her retirement and start a new life.

With their new clarity they could see they were taking each others actions personally. They realized that deep down it was a fear of being loved, and in love, that was at the root of their battle. As they both were able to rise above the pain and hurt, they reconnected to their vision for a loving supportive relationship. Throughout the weekend, they learned more skills for staying connected and working through their conflicts.

Compromise for Love

They were amazed at how lost each had become because they feared losing love. Freeman had seen someone he loved just turn and walk away; and that continued to be his biggest fear. Trudy's past history had intruded on her current life and caused her to react and shut her heart.

The retreat had given them a break from their environment to wake-up and realize what they were reacting to. For Trudy, it wasn't Freeman or giving up her home, she was confronting old vows, and promises she had made herself. She had promised herself she would never give herself away to another man. Now she realized she had to give up those old vows, in order to move forward and make decisions based on what was best for her now.

End of Struggle and Power Play

They now realized how to assist each other to heal, rather than continue power struggles and control games. Love, and deepening their love, was their focus and priority, and directed their choices. The few weeks they spent in fear and pain was a wake up call and turning point for them.

Love's Secret by Trudy and Freeman

Learn from your past, apply the lessons learned, and quit running from hurt and pain. This frees you to grow beyond it, rather than playing victim to it.

Once you have love inside, you have a gift to share with your life partner.

Gratitude builds a foundation to keep love, excitement, and passion alive and thriving.

Your commitment, vision, and love habits empower you to create love, and leave hurt and pain behind.

Love's Secret "Golden Rules"

Congratulations on making positive life changes and choosing to create a deep heart connection with the one you love. Follow our list below to deepen your love and create more "love" habits. Use this list for your *Heart Connections* manual and add your own.

❧ *Look in the mirror and love the person you see. Stay present each day and "fire your inner critic." Focus on one thing each day that you love about yourself. As you learn to focus love to yourself you can then learn to focus love to your mate.*

❧ *Stay present and learn to stop your "inner chatter." Become comfortable with being silent and listen inside. Make a connection to your inner wisdom and then put it into action. This will fill your life with inner peace. You can then learn to direct your energy and thoughts, and become one of only 5% of our society who can choose thoughts and affect their reality.*

❧ *Know what you want and direct your energy toward it. See, feel, and give thanks for having what you want in your life.*

❧ *Make time in your schedule to have fun. Laugh and dance often. Laughter lightens the heart.*

❧ *Your experiences have made you who you are. Learn to embrace what you love from your past and change what has no joy for you. Stay present, choose your reactions to life, and create "inner happiness and inner joy."*

❧ *Anger and love are two opposing forces; they cannot exist in a loving relationship. Forgiveness supports your love habits. Resentment and blame are conditioned childhood responses that push love away. Let go of the past and learn to react with the habit of forgiveness. Forgiveness creates a pathway to keep your heart open and deepen your love. (Refer back to Chapter 9: Inner Life Review.)*

❧ *Practice the habit of being grateful daily and develop a grateful heart. Keep a "Gratitude Journal" every day for a month. Look at how your life changes at the end of the month. Look back over your journal and notice your attitude and your health.*

Differences between you and your mate are the icing on the cake and generally what drew you together. If you were attracted to someone who is just like you, you would grow tired of that person.

Write in your journal each day, and include a list of the things that you appreciate about yourself and your partner. Notice how easy it is to acknowledge these things. Focusing on good things in each of you creates energy to expand what you love.

Anger robs you of moments of joy. Never go to bed with unresolved anger. Stay current with your emotions and be committed to work out disagreements. Learning to communicate and work out disagreements is mandatory to making love.

Love's Secret Heart Connection Album

The following is a fun project that can be shared and supports your vision. It creates pathways for communicating and deepening your love.

Buy a three-inch binder and fill it with page protectors. Design a cover or put a picture of the two of you on your first date, marriage ceremony or some happy occasion.

❦ Once your cover is designed, print and date it.

❦ Insert your commitment signed by each of you.

❦ Make a copy of your budget and insert it. Include a page of your goals and dreams.

❦ Insert your unified vision for your relationship.

❦ Create a collage of happy moments from your pictures.

❦ Insert lists of what makes each of you happy. If possible, take some pictures of times when you have given those things to each other. Add to this monthly.

Copy the Golden Rules, from *Love's Secret* and add your own, to keep your relationship growing and flourishing.

❁

In order to keep on track with your courting schedule and love rituals, keep a page of special moments. This will encourage you to keep adding new pages and come up with exciting moments to share. This keeps the passion alive and growing. Refer to the next chapter for *Love Rituals* or the coupon book for more ideas. This manual not only keeps you on track but will in the future become a special gift for your children.

Make a "courting schedule" and insert it in your manual. In this schedule alternate between the two of you and include dates that you both love.

Love's Secret number eleven
RITUALS OF LOVE

*C*eremonies create sacred space; **Rituals of Love** are a way
of entering spiritual realms together and allowing everything
outside this space, to fall away.

*Each time you enter a sacred space with the intent to deepen
your love, it becomes easier to connect soul-to-soul.*

-ANNIE LAWRENCE

Rituals For Building Love Energy

Rituals create a sacred place for building and nurturing love. In order to keep the spirit of love alive and
strong, include these rituals weekly.

❧ Court your mate long beyond the passionate period of
dating with our love's secret rituals, and keep the fires of
passion glowing.

❧ Rituals build excitement, create passion, and deepen
your love connection.

Love's Secret Number 11 is to practice love rituals weekly with your partner. Your rituals need not be elaborate or

time-consuming: they need to be authentic and come from your heart. The best way is to alternate between partners, keeping each partner active and participating. Once you schedule a ritual, make sure you follow through. Flow from your heart and share your love.

Your goal is to continue dating throughout the life of your relationship, keeping passion and excitement alive and flourishing. Dates used to be planned, and included all the key ingredients needed for your rituals. Once the hunting (or chase) ended and you felt you had snared your target, it was easy to stop the pursuit of love and lose the passion that comes from the chase. The chase is not needed but don't allow boredom to start a habit of taking your love for granted.

Key ingredients are needed for your love rituals. Go back to your individual journals, and find what your partner enjoys receiving within the relationship. Find what was missing as a child and never received; weave these things into your rituals. Below you will find examples of our favorite rituals. We share these to spark your enthusiasm, and offer ideas to create your own magic rituals. Open your heart and your mind, turn off the TV, cellphone, and computer, and let your imagination and passion soar.

In each of the following rituals you will be acquiring important tools for all relationships. Give yourself permission to play with your partner and let laughter lighten your heart.

Within each ritual you will learn habits of being open and receptive, and giving deeply to the one you love. Give from an open heart and be open to receive.

Creating a Sacred Bedroom

Look around your bedroom and make sure it speaks of intimacy and love. Everywhere you look you want to see a reflection of love, and only things that invoke and expand feelings of love.

No clutter, no TVs, no computers or office should be allowed. The bedroom is your sacred space for love set up just for you and your partner. Make sure that it has positive feelings, and is a warm and inviting place for both of you.

Creating a sacred bedroom is a commitment to your mate. It is the sacred ground to nourish and feed your love and passion. Clutter and work dampen this space and rob you of the passion and pleasure you deserve.

Once you have created a sacred space in your bedroom, keep it clean.

If you have an old mattress that has been with you through another relationship, get rid of it. The mattress holds energy; you want the mattress clear and free of any negative energy of the past. Even if it is a stretch financially, make it a priority. Your mattress is not only where you get your rest and rejuvenation, it is the foundation of your relationship. Invest here before anywhere else, including music, art, and all the amenities.

Sacred Bedroom Space Enhancements

Make a love alter in your love corner, far right corner as you stand looking into the room. On this altar include something that depicts love to you (check our website for our love altar kit). Include a picture of you and your mate. In this picture, make sure it depicts the love you feel for each other. A rose quartz crystal is another good choice for your alter.

Include a green plant somewhere in the room and keep it healthy.

On the day of your love ritual, put on clean sheets (try red sheets to create the fire of passion), vacuum, and dust. Prepare your room for the most valued friend that you have ever known. Spray the sheets with a passion spray. Our passion spray includes rose water, patchouli, neroli, sandalwood, and ylang-ylang, make your own or order it from us on line.

Once a day give your partner a special hug while being totally present and focused on your love. Create excitement by leaving love notes on the bathroom mirror. Say how much you enjoyed last night, or how much you are looking forward to tonight. Little things are the magic potions that sparked the fire of passion. Keep the fire lit and blazing.

If you have been busy and preoccupied, pull yourself

back and surprise your mate. Create an unplanned and unexpected date or ritual. Give your mate a massage. Have an evening where you are attentive and giving to your mate. Enjoy giving without expecting a return or specific outcome.

Create a trouble tree, before you enter your home hang your troubles on it. Leave your troubles outside your home and especially outside the bedroom. Never allow yourself to bring up problems or disagreements in the bedroom. Remember the *Golden Rule for Love* and never go to bed upset with each other.

Love's Secret Coupon Book

In this book be sure to include all the things that you love to receive from each other.

Create a schedule to redeem at least one coupon per week. Below find some favorites to include, but be sure to come up with your own favorites.

‍ Free, passionate foot massage.

‍ Breakfast in bed.

‍ Sensuous massage.

‍ Love genie for one day, whatever you want.

‍ Day off to be alone.

‍ Getaway of your choice, three days of your choice.

‍ Love ritual bath.

‍ Night out on the town.

🝆 Kissin' and lovin' session to last at least one hour.

🝆 Love coupon for one quickie: to be redeemed upon request.

🝆 One free wish.

🝆 One hour of cuddling-spooning-breathing together.

🝆 One "heart expression" session.

🝆 Walk in Nature.

Love Bath Ritual

In ancient cultures, the bath was a form of foreplay used to relax and open channels of love and passion.

You may choose this ritual for either partner. Do your research and find just the right scented candle (your mate's favorite scent), add the perfect aroma to the bath (choose a scent that enhances and elicits passion), and add your partner's favorite music.

Prepare a safe, sacred space. Light candles, burn incense, turn off phones, and put on some calm, relaxing music. Say a prayer to have the space filled and infused with love, guidance, healing, and peace.

🝆 Light candles to set the mood for love.

🝆 Place flowers in the bedroom.

🝆 Fill the bath with warm water and add passionate aromatherapy oil. Supply a pillow for your partner's head.

◖ Place a stereo in the bathroom with their favorite CD playing.

◖ Set a timer and leave your partner alone to soak for 15 minutes. Before you leave them alone, share passionate kisses to set the mood. No more than 15 minutes, the intent is to relax not nod off to sleep.

◖ Wash your mate's body. Massage their neck, and shoulders. Breathe deeply. The next step is up to you. You know how to build the passionate fire and then how to complete with intimate bliss.

The Yellow Flower Ritual

The intention of this ritual is to enhance a heart connection then afterward to share communication from the heart.

Prepare a safe, sacred space. Light candles, burn incense, turn off phones, and put on some calm relaxing music. Say a prayer to have the space filled and infused with love, guidance, healing, and peace.

◖ Sitting on the floor, the first partner gets comfortable using pillows for support if necessary.

◖ The second partner sits gently on the first with legs wrapped around the partner's hips.

◖ This ritual can be done without clothing. Just sit looking deeply into one another's eyes.

◖ Focus your thoughts on love, and relax more deeply by

practicing long, deep breathing. Hold thoughts of the things that you love most about your mate.

❦ Breathe deeply and synchronize your breathing, in and out, relaxing and allowing yourself to melt into your partner.

❦ You will feel fires of passion begin to build. This is good and may be acted on later, but for now continue the breathing for at least 10 minutes.

❦ Once the 10 minutes have elapsed, sit apart and continue looking deeply into one another's eyes.

After the ritual share your individual impressions and insights. If you are having disagreements, this is a good ceremony to do to clear the air before entering your bedroom.

When you have disagreements speak from your heart and say what and how you are feeling. Ask for what you want from your partner. Be gentle and avoid blaming and projecting your own hurt and discomfort on your partner.

Heart Encounter Ritual

This ritual is similar to the above yellow flower ceremony, except this time sitting across from each other.

Prepare a safe, sacred space. Light candles, burn incense, turn off phones, and put on some calm relaxing music. Say a prayer to have the space filled and infused with love, guidance, healing, and peace.

☙ Synchronize your breathing, as you gently and softly gaze into each other's eyes.

☙ See your partner as a child sitting in front of you.

☙ Gaze into their eyes, and allow their soul or spirit to guide you to their history.

☙ Journey back to your mate's childhood. Communicate with him or her as a child and send lots of love.

☙ Invite the child to share their story with you and just listen quietly inside. This communication will not be like communicating with someone in person but rather you will sense the child's response.

☙ What was it that they wanted as a child and never got?

☙ Hold an intention to help them heal their inner child and bring the child into their heart.

☙ Ask your mate's inner child to teach you how to play, and laugh, and have fun together.

Listen and be open for a dialogue to open between you and their inner child. Don't force it; just allow it to happen. This is a great way to gain perspective of each other's history and patterns.

EFT Heart to Heart Communication

The following is a technique, using EFT to release the emotional charge before you have a "heart-expression" session. This is good training to help you open your heart and establish good communication skills. With practice, you will feel safe to deal with issues before they become emotionally charged.

Prepare a safe, sacred space. Light candles, burn incense, turn off phones, and put on some calm relaxing music. Say a prayer to have the space filled and infused with love, guidance, healing, and peace

Either in chairs or on the floor sit facing each other. Synchronize your breathing for 5 minutes and concentrate on the most positive things you can think of about your mate. Once you have established a heart connection, feel where you are storing an emotional charge in your body. Whatever comes to mind first, anger, hurt, sadness, or fear.

Once you feel an emotion in your body, see if you can name it, like frustration. The person who is feeling the highest charge begins.

First find a point on the top of the head, the soft spot. Each partner will tap and repeat the words and phrases together. Before you begin check in and find how much emotional charge you are feeling? Use a scale of 0-10 (0 being no emotional charge and 10 being the maximum level).

After you finish the round of tapping and words and phrases check the scale again and see if the emotions have lightened. If not, do another round and add any phrases that may have surfaced inside either of you. Continue until the "emotions scale" is down to zero.

❧ **Both partners tap on the top of the head and repeat,**"Even though I feel this hurt in my chest, still I deeply and completely love myself and accept myself, and choose to release this hurt and surprise myself by keeping my heart open."

❧ **Move the tapping down to the points on the inside of each eyebrow, above the bridge of the nose. Partners repeat,** "Even though I feel this tightness in my chest and I want to shut down and move away from you, still I deeply and completely love myself and accept myself and choose to keep my heart open and surprise myself with how easy it is to share my feelings and let the hurt go."

❧ **The tapping moves to the temples. Partners repeat,**"Even though I feel hurt when you don't listen to me when I ask you to do something to help me around the house, still I deeply and completely love and accept myself and choose to keep my heart open and keep communicating my needs, and surprise myself with how easy it is to keep my heart open."

❧ **Move the tapping to each side of the nostrils just above the upper lip. Partners repeat,**"Even though I have anger and hurt surfacing from when I was a child, because I never felt heard by my parents, or that what I wanted mattered, and I am reacting as if you were my parent, still I choose to deeply and completely, love myself and accept myself and breath deeply, keep my heart open, and surprise myself with how easy it is to speak from my heart, ask for what I want, and let the hurt go."

☾ **Move tapping to just below nose on center of upper lip. Partners repeat,**"Even though I feel (what you are feeling) and still feel this tightness in my chest, still I choose to deeply and completely love myself, accept myself, and choose to keep my heart open, and surprise myself with how easy it is to laugh at myself and have fun with_____, during our disagreements, and stay connected to my love.

☾ **Move tapping down to center of chin.   Partners repeat,**"Even though when I felt hurt as a child I shut down and never learned how to speak up and share my feelings and release my hurt, still I choose to deeply and completely love and accept myself, and choose to keep my heart open, and surprise myself with how easy and fun it is to share my feelings and keep communicating with my partner."

☾ **Move tapping down to the clavicles, two bony notches below chin at upper center of chest. Partners repeat,**"Even though I have habits of shutting down and holding on to hurt to punish my mate and myself, still I choose to deeply and completely love and accept myself and choose to keep my heart open, communicate my needs, and surprise myself with how easy it is to learn new habits that support and deepen our love."

℃ **Move tapping to breast area, just below the breast where the breast meets the chest, this point is between the ribs and tends to be a tender point, and is a point where we usually hold anger toward ourselves and others. Partners repeat,** "Even though I get angry at myself when I shut down and stay stuck in old habits and push love away, still I choose to deeply and completely love and accept myself and choose to keep my heart open and surprise myself with how easy it is to choose love by communicating my needs from my heart."

℃ **Move tapping to point under the arm where the armpit and chest meet. Partners repeat,** "Even though I have old habits that don't support love, still I choose to deeply and completely love and accept myself, and choose to let my old habits go, and surprise myself with how easy it is to choose new habits that deepen our love and heart connection."

Heart Protection Ritual

Prepare a safe, sacred space. Light candles, burn incense, turn off phones, and put on some calm relaxing music. Say a prayer to have the space filled and infused with love, guidance, healing, and peace.

Sit across from each other, and synchronize your

breathing. Alternate talking and listening. The silent partner will just listen, and take the words deeply into (his or her) heart and soul. The partner who is talking will put one hand on the center of the chest of the silent partner, and then place their second hand on top of the silent partner's hand, the silent partner then places their second hand on top.

Talking partner says to silent partner, I will protect your heart. Silent partner listens, allows their heart to respond, and listens to the inner voice to hear whatever comes up. Talking partner continues to chant in a very gentle and loving voice, I will protect your heart. Continue for 10 minutes. Switch partners. Don't share anything until both partners have had a chance to experience being the recipient.

Take turns sharing from your heart. Share for a period of 10-20 minutes what each partner experienced. Finish your experience by sharing either a sensuous foot massage or full body massage.

Sensuous Foot Massage Ritual

Prepare a safe, sacred space. Light candles, burn incense, turn off phones, and put on some calm relaxing music. Say a prayer to have the space filled and infused with love, guidance, healing, and peace.

One partner practices being open and receptive and the other partner is the giver. These roles are both important to master within the relationship and enhance all aspects of the relationship. It is equally important to be able to flow between the roles of receiving deeply and giving deeply with an open heart, with no expectations of outcome.

To increase it's potent effect prepare your love's secret oil ahead of time. Oils that intensify pleasure include rose, rose hip seed, ylang-ylang, sandalwood, neroli, spikenard, and vanilla. You may choose oils that are more therapeutic if a partner has pain or stress. Good choices are peppermint, cinnamon, lavender, and birch. You choose the intention of the foot-massage ritual.

Have the receiver lie back and relax. Begin to massage and work gently on the toes and along the arch which is the spine reflex. Working this area sends messages to the nervous system and the brain to relax and releases endorphins that support the relaxation response in your body/mind.

Your intention is to relax their body and send a message of relaxation to all the nerves, and cells in your partner's body.

The big toe represents the head and neck. Working it will relax their mind, head and neck.

The area just below the toes stimulates the shoulders. Work this well and see the tension normally held in the shoulders begin to dissolve.

After you have massaged the feet and begun the relaxation response, the rest is up to you. The area between the toes tends to be very sensitive and sensuous. Be as soft and gentle as possible there. This is a good area to kiss, lick or be as kinky as you or your partner wish.

Sensuous Massage Ritual

Prepare a safe, sacred space. Light candles, burn incense, turn off phones, and put on some calm relaxing music. Say a prayer to have the space filled and infused with love, guidance, healing, and peace.

Have your partner lie on a clean sheet that you don't mind getting oil on. You may wish to put a pillow under their head. Massage the area in the neck and shoulders. This is the area where 90% of body tension is held.

Once you have relaxed that area, gently massage along the tight-ropey muscles of the spine. This will help release the tension that is constricting blood flow, and begin to send messages of relaxation to all areas of the body.

You may wish to just concentrate on this area. As your partner begins to relax and becomes more open and receptive; the rest is up to you.

You may wish to experiment with feathers, powder, or what ever your mate finds arousing and exciting. Remember to honor what you mate requests. If they are tired and want to go to bed, honor that, too. No expectations, pure giving from the heart, honoring your mate's rhythms, wants and needs!

Love connections are deepened and a firm foundation is built by including these rituals at least once a week. If more attention is put on these simple rituals, and less time and money are spent on extravagances, it will add happiness to your years of partnership. You can then plan for your healthy and happy retirement and long life together.

Love's Secret number twelve
Create Support

*L*ove the life you live, by focusing on love the rest of your life.
  -Annie Lawrence

Create A Support System

Love's Secret Number 12 is to create a support system, and accept assistance, to create your dream life and relationship.

Many of you will be able to embrace new love habits and stop fighting and make love. Others who are more deeply identified with their conditioning, habits, patterns, and thoughts will need help in shifting to new ways of connecting to love. This chapter is written to assist you to create support systems, find mentors, and any assistance needed for support and in times of crisis.

Many new and exciting tools are being offered today, to shift old toxic habits of relating, and to assist you to become a love vibration. There are many beautiful souls who are speaking out and sharing their life's work, to lift old patterns and conditioning of self-hurt, self-abuse, and self-hatred, left by our parents and their parents.

Support for Love

Our technology has advanced by leaps and bounds, and yet our planet and society, as a whole, are still drowning in abuse and pain. It hurts me too much and I have become too sensitive to watch the local news station and the tragedies that are reported daily. Perhaps this is a reminder of old pain and hurt that were too prevalent in my childhood. I give thanks daily for the inner strength and commitment to create new habits and emotions that support my new life of inner peace, happiness, and a love filled marriage.

Hold the Intention to Create A Happy Life

A happy life is truly a blessing, and it does not come to you by chance. It is not guaranteed. Happiness will continue in your life only when you take time, moment-to-moment, to make 'love-habits' a part of your everyday life.

The lessons laid out in *Love's Secret* have you well on your way to creating a new life. During the initial phase, while learning to live life surrounded by peace and happiness, you will experience ups and downs.

As you develop love habits, surround yourself with like-minded couples, support groups, and mentors. Reach out when you need help. Don't waste precious happy moments stuck in pain.

The saddest experience we have at our retreat center

is seeing couples who have suffered in pain for years. Not knowing how to get relief. We feel especially blessed when they leave happy and reconnected to love.

Create a Supportive Environment

Clear your environment of friends and family members who support the opposite of what you want in your life. Letting go of family members is a challenging commitment for most of you, but remember they are a negative reinforcement tool for your old habits. It is very hard to look at your interactions with your family and see clearly how they reinforce destructive, personal habits.

Even though you have been removing toxic patterns and habits, they are deeply embedded in your subconscious mind, and easily triggered by family members. When you find yourself automatically reacting within your daily life with co-workers, friends, and your partner, don't panic. Realize that at times you will react, don't give your power away by beating yourself up.

People who support inner peace and encourage the state of happiness and joy are good choices to include in your life. After you are stronger, you will be able to feel inner peace no matter who you are around, or what environment.

Set boundaries and cut ties with friends and family, who leave you feeling depleted, and full of guilt. We all grow and change at different rates. Some of your family and friends will never grow or change in this lifetime. They will stay stuck in their self-destructive habits.

That is their choice and we have to accept that. A main principal of life is that we each have self-choice. You must honor each person's choice and take responsibility for your own life and the choices you make.

Seek Support in Like-minded Groups

Your first step in creating a support group is to seek out a group of friends who are like-minded. There are many ways to find these friends: through hiking, biking, gardening, or dance groups. There are yoga, meditation, Tai Chi, Qigong, *A Course in Miracles*, *Compassionate Communication*, and Reiki share groups. Whatever your interests, there is a group to support it. All of these groups are working toward creating more inner peace and harmony. Once you agree on a focus, you will be led to places to connect with other couples. Your support group of couples will also value their relationship, and be actively investing time and energy to create lasting heart connections and lifetime partnerships.

Consider spiritual organizations, and churches that focus on lifting the old paradigms of limiting beliefs. Each organization has its own formula for focusing on positive thoughts and clearing the past and destructive belief systems. Sometimes you will find counselors within the church or organization, along with prayer support groups. Your goal is to find someone you trust, whom you can talk with, and who will help you stay focused on creating a lifelong partnership.

Avoid making your sounding board a friend or family member. They may help you feel supported, but may have reasons of their own to support distancing, rather than choosing love and connections.

It is not unusual for them to have the same patterns and habits that you have, and of course, they will validate your feelings. They will also support self-destructive habits of pulling away, holding onto hurt and perpetuating right/wrong attitudes, rather than choosing resolution.

Friends and family have no training in seeing into your patterns, and may have a negative pay-off in helping you to choose to feel hurt and distancing your mate. They may feel threatened by seeing you change and grow, and may fear losing your love.

Find a Mentor, Coach or Counselor

Reach out to someone who has the knowledge and happiness that you want to create in your own life. Notice how you feel when you interview someone for a mentor, coach, or counselor; make sure you leave the session feeling up lifted. Are they calm, do they project the inner-peace and confidence that you want to bring into your own life?

Your goal and intention is to find someone who walks

his or her talk. Make sure they are not offering advice that they promote, rather than truly live. Use the same criteria for finding couples with whom you want to develop friendships. Set up support systems that echo the lifestyle you want to embrace.

Once you choose an activity group of like-minded couples, you are actively creating two new habits. A group of like-minded couples supports focus on inner peace. At the same time it offers new ways of enjoying your life together. These activities are fun and enjoyable and are a great way to exercise, stay fit, and have fun together. Creating good health throughout your life is always a goal, and sharing these activities is another way of bonding with your mate.

Once you have found your support systems and activities, and make choices that support love and deepen intimacy, you are focused on your path. Does this mean there will never be disagreements, and that there will only be happy moments? I wish this were the case. But unfortunately our lives are about commitment, consistently working things out, and compromise.

Stay Open to Growth

Just when you think you have the formula perfected, a new level of hurt may pop up to be healed and released. This is what relationships are about: constant change, growth, and each person unfolding to be the best you can be. New parts of yourselves are constantly being revealed. This means peeling back old hurt and pain, layer by layer.

I have been working on myself consciously for over thirty years and still have present day events trigger old painful memories. Today it is easier to spot pain and heal old patterns of reacting, and make new choices. But my journey of growth and change continues daily.

Resources Offered through Retreat and Heal

If you go to www.retreatandheal.com you will find resources and services offered through *Retreat and Heal*. We offer support for couples and relationships through couple's retreats, EFT, hypnotherapy, and phone consultations. Our website has a full list of these services, costs, and dates offered.

Our retreats are available in Arizona, California, and Hawaii offering couples retreats, group retreats, corporate retreats and special retreats. Please contact us to sign up for our newsletter. Send us your story of how Love's Secret helped your life and relationship. You may submit questions and feedback to info@retreatandheal.com. Please address your comments to *Love's Secret* attention: Annie. I love to hear from you! Due to the volume of inquiries and feedback we receive, it may take a few days to respond, so please be patient.

I wish you good luck with your journey. My prayer is that your heart connection stays strong with yourself and your life partner. My hope is that your life be blessed with inner peace, financial freedom, and ever-deepening levels of love. My wish is that you find your passion within and direct it into your relationship and your life purpose. Stretch your self-imposed limits and dare to dream dreams of happiness, fulfillment, and ecstatic bliss. Then wake up to find these dreams are your reality.

Peaceful Blessings

-ANNIE

Appendix A
RETREAT INFORMATION

How do I find out more about Retreat and Heal?

www.retreatandheal.com

How do I choose a Retreat?

Make a list of what you are looking for in a retreat program. Ask lots of questions. Does the retreat facilitator have experience in working with the issues that you wish to address? Make sure that you have plenty of time to reflect during your retreat program. The real meaning of retreat is to stop and turn inward. Therefore, quietness and stillness are very important.

What types of retreats do you offer?

We offer three different types of retreats. Couples group retreats, corporate retreats, and our inner healing personal retreats.

Where are the retreats offered?

Our *Inner Healing Retreats* are offered year round in

Sedona, Arizona. The *Corporate Retreats* are also offered in Sedona, and must be scheduled 3-4 weeks in advance. Our retreats fill up fast so call ahead. The *Couple's Retreats* are offered in Sedona, Arizona; Warner Springs, California, and Hawaii. The *Couple's Retreats* are booked up six months to a year ahead, so plan early.

Highlights of our Couple's Retreat

Spend time in a beautiful environment with other couples who are working to create deeper heart connections. Enjoy time alone with your mate, with your coach, and group-time perfecting your love skills. You will create a 'love commitment,' a 'vision for love,' and a *Heart Connections* manual. Learn skills for communicating and negotiating to create more harmony and joy in your relationship. When you complete this retreat you will feel your love and heart connection renewed and strengthened.

Inner Healing Personal Retreats

Enjoy the beauty of Sedona, and spend contemplative time alone. Receive massages, vortex ceremonies, hikes, meditations, hypnotherapy and EFT to clear your blocks to inner peace and personal power. You will leave feeling refreshed and renewed.

Corporate Day Retreats in the beauty of Sedona, Arizona.

Let us design a day retreat just for your group. We will spend the day in nature with the beauty of the red rocks and utilize effective tools like EFT, hypnotherapy, and drumming, to remove the blocks to success and build team spirit and group harmony. Some effective team building methods in nature can include treasure hunts, labyrinth walks, and hikes in nature. We will reconnect your group to their hearts, integrity, and inner wisdom to create a more effective and harmonious team. Day retreats also include corporate massage. Your team will finish our day retreat refreshed and realigned with their passion ready to meet and exceed their goals.

Appendix B
EFT Tools

*E*FT or Emotional Freedom Technique is an effective tool for clearing emotional energy. This technique includes tapping on nine major points that correlate to the energy meridians that traverse the body. When we either deny or ignore emotions, that we are uncomfortable with, these emotions get stuck and cause both emotional and physical reactions.

In this appendix you will find a chart that shows the nine points used throughout the book. You will also find this chart listed on our site for free download. For more extensive information and DVD's offered by the creator of EFT you will also find a link to his website. There you will also find a link for a free download for the basic manual for applying EFT.

One of Gary Craig's (founder of EFT) favorite sayings is "try it on everything, it just might be a one minute miracle". This means that EFT works for almost everything including breaking habits of overeating, becoming smoke free, weight loss, headache relief, pain relief, and relief from depression. It is quickly becoming the favorite self-help remedy to apply rather than popping a pill. Pills and medication numb emotions but do not bring lasting relief and is not a cure. EFT is free, easy to apply, and will surprise you how effective it is. We have applied the technique to hundreds of clients and retreat guests and have seen good consistent results. After just a couple of sessions our guests feel confident to apply EFT for themselves.

Emotional Freedom Tapping Points

1. Top of the center of the head where the soft spot would be.

2. On the inner corner of each eye brow.

3. Soft spot on the temples, on each side.

4. Under the eyes on the cheek bones.

5. On each side of the nostril.

6. Center of the upper lip.

7. Just below the bottom lip, center of the chin.

8. Underneath the clavicles.

9. Under the armpits on each side.

Emotional Freedom Tapping Points
illustration

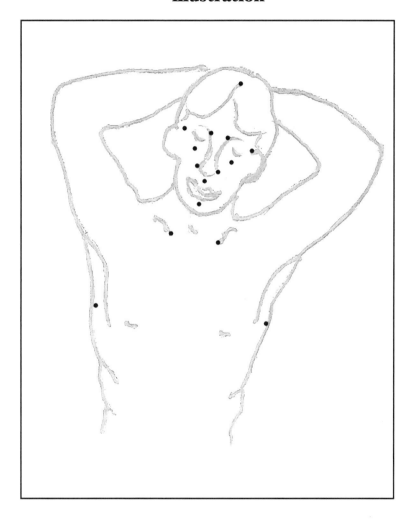

INDEX*

[Created with **TExtract** / www.Texyz.com]